Foundations of a Moral Government

SAMUEL RUTHERFORD'S *LEX, REX*

A NEW ANNOTATED VERSION IN STANDARD ENGLISH

Michael A. Milton

TANGLEWOOD
PUBLISHING

Foundations of a Moral Government

BY MICHAEL A. MILTON

Permission to use pictures and annotations of the life of Samuel Rutherford
granted by Crich Baptist Church, Crich, Derbyshire, UK

Book design and layout Mieke Moller & Laura Rodriguez
Cover layout and design by Christy Rodriguez

Printed in the United States of America

For my wife, who has joined me in
serving Church and State
to protect those cherished liberties
and bind them forever
to the Word of God.

And to my son, John Michael who,
with all of our children,
and the rising generations after them,
must spend and be spent in guarding
what has been entrusted to all as
a priceless treasure.

To the legacy of my forefather,
Reverend Isham Milton (1760-1834),
who fought in the American Revolutionary War,
with his brothers, through my father,
Jesse Ellis Milton (1908-1964)
who commanded troop transports in World War Two
through deadly North Atlantic U-boat-infested-waters
for the inalienable rights that Rutherford exposited
from the Holy Scriptures;

To the glory of God the Father, God the Son,
and God the Holy Spirit
who allowed this filthy sinner saved by grace
to proclaim the Gospel
he once blasphemed.

But a reverence for our great Creator, principles of humanity, and the dictates of common sense, must convince all those who reflect upon the subject, that government was instituted to promote the welfare of mankind, and ought to be administered for the attainment of that end.

— *Declaration of the Causes and Necessity of Taking up Arms,*
July 6, 1775, A Declaration by the Representatives of the United Colonies of North-America [sic], Now Met in Congress at Philadelphia, setting forth the Causes and Necessity of Their Taking up Arms.

———

Stand fast therefore in the liberty wherewith Christ hath made us free and be not entangled again with the yoke of bondage.

— Galatians 5:1, 1599 Geneva Bible

Table of Contents

Lex, Rex

Acknowledgments

The Genesis for this book began with the 2017 conversation between me and the Reverend Charles Rodriguez of Fortress Books. What if there could be an annotated version of Samuel Rutherford's great treaties on ecclesiastical and political theory: *Lex, Rex*? The project, at first, seemed easy enough. Get a copy of the document. Read through it. Give some commentary. Right. You would think I would know better by now. Each and every section of Rutherford demanded a considerable amount of research into both the specific situation he was addressing as well as the context of the dispute. Rutherford was an unsurpassed scholar. His work is replete with not only Biblical references, but classical ones, as well. Having done work in seventeenth-century historical theology I felt somewhat prepared to go into this. Having done postdoctoral work at the University of North Carolina at Chapel Hill in public policy and government, as part of my senior officer education with the United States Army Reserve, I was comfortable with the topic. Faith and public policy has long been an interest of mine. It seems to grab the headlines every day. Yet, none of that truly prepared me for what was to come. What I begin to realize, rather quickly, was that this was one of the major undertakings of my literary career. Not only did the labor involve the research already mentioned, it required that I condense my thoughts to just a few paragraphs, sometimes merely a few lines for the end-of-chapter annotation. As any preacher will tell you it is exceedingly more difficult to compose a short homily than a full-length expository sermon. That is what it felt like in working on this project. Yes, I was in over my head. I needed help. And help came.

I thank Dr. George Grant, my longtime friend, and a man who prays for me, writes me, and has encouraged me through many trials.

"A friend is always loyal, and a brother is born to help in time of need" (Proverbs 17:17, NLT).

I want to thank my personal assistant, Mrs. Christine Hartung. Her cheerful and efficient administrative support allowed me to work on this volume while also shepherding a local parish ministry, designing courses and teaching at Erskine Theological Seminary, writing for several periodicals, and providing pastoral counseling to ministers, students, Chaplains, and hurting people in our community seeking guidance from God's Word and through the power of the Holy Spirit. Just writing these words reminds me of how valuable her services are. Yet, this Charlotte policeman's wife and godly mother conducts her daily work of ministry support with a lovely Christian demeanor that adds something imminently more meaningful to her title, "Assistant to Dr. Milton." That just doesn't even begin to describe what she does! Thank you, Christine.

I want to thank the faculty and staff of Erskine Theological Seminary as they supported me in this work. When I was down in my health, Erskine offered me a place to minister. Frequently, I have to "give-in" to the effects of a disease out of my control. When I call in to say, "I'm down for the count," my colleagues invariably respond, "We love you! We are praying for you!" You can't beat that, can you? What a wonderful place to minister.

The congregation of Trinity Chapel Presbyterian Church (ARP), a new church development in the Weddington, North Carolina community, prayed for me during this project. Being a new church development, we have our work cut out for us without adding a monumental undertaking such as the essential guide to a moral democracy! Our core group members are very gracious to their old founding pastor. I am appreciative for Professor Don Piers II, Director of Music at Trinity Chapel. Don is a friend that reminds me of the faithfulness of Christ Jesus. He is a musician that reminds me of the grand company of church musicians through the years who have conducted with skill and spirit. Thanks, as well, to our church planting apprentice and intern, Mr. Keith Ginn. I trust that by the time this is published Keith will join the college of ordained ministers of Word and Sacrament. I pray the Lord will use him mightily in the years to come.

I must add a special thank you to John Michael, my son, who helped me through some difficult physical days. I have said it before: He has literally picked me up and put me to bed during difficult times of my illness. He still does. Son, pretty soon we have to stop this! But, I love the heart of a godly young man that I see in you. I am thankful to the Lord for your sweet spirit. You are also an able historian!

As I was working on this I was also in the midst of retirement from the United States Army reserve. After 32 years of service I had reached the mandatory age to complete that wonderful chapter in my life. It was actually 41 years ago that I raised my right hand and took an oath of allegiance, not to a person, but to an idea. I realize how important Samuel Rutherford's Biblical exegesis and exposition remains as I also recall with thanksgiving those Soldiers, Sailors, Guardsmen, Airmen, Marines, Coast Guardsmen, and Merchant Mariners (and their families) who put it all on the line. I love those service members. It has been the honor of my life to have served you as a Chaplain. May the Lord bless you as you defend the ideas laid forth in this volume.

I always save the best for last. And the best, and the first and always, is my wife, Mae. Thank you, Mae, not merely for what you do but even more for who you are. I love you. "When people hear me, what they never see is the deepest part of my life; Thank God for the pastor's wife."

"An excellent wife who can find? She is far more precious than jewels" (Proverbs 31:10 ESV).

I thank our King of Kings who saved this filthy-sinner-by-grace and called him to preach the unsearchable riches of Jesus Christ that he once blasphemed.

M.A.M.

Foreword

JOHN M. FRAME

A few years ago I was looking forward to working with Mike Milton in my capacity as a theology professor and his capacity as Chancellor and CEO of Reformed Theological Seminary. I appreciated his ministry and his vision for theological education. But God's strange providence intervened. Mike was hit with a serious illness that led to his resignation from the seminary. I prayed that God would enable him to continue his theological leadership in some form, but I did not know him well enough to guess what form that work would take.

Well, even then I should have known better than I did that Mike was hugely gifted in many areas. As the Vita at the end of this volume indicates, he has spent 32 years in military service, first as a linguist, then as a chaplain. He has been a pastor and has done significant work in historical scholarship. Now I have learned that he has specialized in the study of Samuel Rutherford (1600-1661), the great Scottish theologian who influenced the work of the Westminster Assembly and indeed the whole subsequent course of Reformed theology.

Rutherford's greatest writing was *Lex, Rex*, which should perhaps be translated "the Law is King," or "the King is under the Law." That is, in any case, the main thesis of this momentous work. As such, it became subsequently a major influence on political thought, not only among Presbyterians, but on the philosophical developments that led to the founding documents of the United States of America. The work of John Locke is arguably indebted to Rutherford, as is the work of Edmund Burke and that of the Rev. John Witherspoon, pastor and President of Princeton University, who signed the American Declaration of Independence. Therefore Rutherford, the fountainhead of this development, is important to all our current discussion about the liberty of the citizen and the powers of government.

Rutherford was mainly concerned with opposing the "divine right of kings" as that doctrine was presented in his time. On that doctrine, the authority of kings was given directly by God, without any collaboration by the citizens he rules. That doctrine was already contrary to the British tradition embodied in the Magna Carta. But some continued to defend it as a distinctly theistic and biblical doctrine of governance. Rutherford, with a deeper understanding of Scripture than his opponents, opposed this notion. A truly biblical doctrine of government is not merely the assertion that God is the source of rule. Rather, we must look carefully at how God confers authority on governments, according to the Bible. Rutherford insisted that in Scripture God installs kings (even kings like David whom he personally warrants by anointing) by the actions of people. Though David was anointed as a young man, he did not actually begin to rule Judah (and later Israel) until the elders of God's people concurred in his selection.

So although Rutherford emphasizes the authority of God over the state, he is known as the champion of the popular mandate and the rights of citizens over against the ruler. In his view, one can and should advocate a distinctively biblical political system without the divine right of kings and with strong checks and balances against the abuses of authority.

These are two emphases that must be heard today. First, we need to hear God's word, in the area of politics as much as in everything else. The idea that politics is a secular discipline and should be divorced from religion is a grave mistake. Without God, our politics becomes autonomous, subject to every wild fantasy of undisciplined human minds. In the present American political dialogue, the new socialism is the extreme of this development, proposals to spend trillions upon trillions of money we do not have on enormous increases in the size and authority of government, an idolatry of the state that even the defenders of the divine right of kings could not have imagined.

Second, we need to hear Rutherford's call for the liberty of citizens. The founders of the American system listened carefully to Rutherford's advice that there be checks and balances on all the branches of government, that no branch should ever claim absolute (divine) authority and that none should ever transgress the rights of the people, rights given not by the authority of the state but by God himself. Recognizing the authority of God means recognizing the legitimate authority of the state, but also the liberty of the people from the state in their inalienable rights.

Rutherford's book is, like all books of its time, written in language that is difficult for modern people to understand. We owe many thanks to Mike Milton for careful work, analyzing and paraphrasing Rutherford for modern readers. He has used well his gifts as a linguist, a pastor, and a theological scholar. As we endure this historical period of radically divisive political debate, it is hard to imagine a better gift to the American people than this restoration of Rutherford's important work.

John M. Frame, PhD
Prof. Emeritus of Systematic Theology and Philosophy
Reformed Theological Seminary
Orlando, FL

Preface

MICHAEL A. MILTON

Some books are burned. Some books burn. Some books do both. *Lex, Rex* by Samuel Rutherford is that kind of book. *Lex, Rex*, a rejoinder to another book, *Sacro-sancta regum majestas:* or, *The Sacred and Royal Prerogative of Christian Kings* by "J.A." (The author identified as John Maxwell [c.1590-1647]). It may be that Maxwell lit the match with his opening question and answer:

> "Quaestio prima. Whether or not, the King be only and immediately dependent from God, and independent from the Body of the People, diffusive, collective, representative, or virtual?
> WE hold the Affirmative, that the King is only and immediately dependent from Almighty God, the King of Kings, and Lord of Lords, and independent in his Sovereignty and Power, from the Community in what Notion so ever you conceive it . . ."

Maxwell argued, with force of emotion, Biblical and classical citation, and with what he described as "Reverend Antiquity, and sound Reasons asserted," "The King is the Law. He is appointed by God. He is answerable to God alone."

Today, it is hard to believe that an Englishman would say such a thing. That is because Rutherford's response not only refuted it but recovered the sound mindedness of the Magna Carta. English law is settled on such limits of government and governors.

In seventeenth-century England, an autocratic understanding of monarchy had both civil and ecclesiastical meaning for those who proposed it and those who refuted it. So, yes, John Maxwell lit the match. But it was Rutherford who fanned an otherwise diminutive flame into a raging conflagration. "No!" Rutherford responded. And the Scottish Presbyterian minister and professor went on to demonstrate with scholarly care, razor-sharp intellect, and prophetic mastery of both Holy Scripture in the original languages and the classics of Western Democracy (Rutherford is notable for his ease in handling direct quotes, references, or allusions to Aristotle's Politics, Metaphysics, Rhetoric; the great Westminster divine was well acquainted with Thomas Aquinas):

"The King is not above the law. Governors are made by and are accountable to the Governed. Such human governance and limitations of civil authority are both proven by Natural Law and taught in Scripture."

Lex, Rex was much more than a scholarly polemic (though the professor from the University of Edinburgh could certainly hold his own in that arena). Samuel Rutherford's 44 questions and answers about the divine rights of Kings and the rule of law set nations ablaze. The fire of Rutherford's response in *Lex, Rex* was not merely a little brushfire in the larger field of democracy. Rutherford's masterpiece of life and liberty grounded in God and His revelations, creative and providential, laid the foundation for the rights of the governed ever since. His contribution simply cannot be overestimated.

The truth is Samuel Rutherford never rejected monarchy though he rejected absolute monarchy as jus divina (by divine right). Rev. Dr. Rutherford actually considered the monarchical form of government most like the divine governance of God through Jesus Christ. Yet, the high-octane principles which the seventeenth-century Westminster divine unleashed were just too combustible to limit to the question of a constitutional monarchy in the British Isles. Rutherford's ideas were also too popular to limit to Scotland, England, Wales, and Ireland. *Lex, Rex* became a steaming stone skipping across the North Atlantic, splintering into white-hot shrapnel, embedding itself into the civic and political landscape of the New World. The searing shreds of Rutherford's doctrine stirred the souls of the Americans. From the frosty winters of the Connecticut River Valley to the balmy tidewater marshes of Jamestown, Virginia, and across the seminal decades of the American experience, theologians and philosophers like Jonathan Edwards, as well as political upstarts like Patrick Henry, gathered up what they believed to be sacred stones of scriptural self-governance. In the case of those like Patrick Henry the 44 questions and the 44 decisive, transformative answers and Rutherford's civic catechism became more like five smooth stones in David's ammunition sack. All of this is to say that Samuel Rutherford's *Lex, Rex* became one of the single most influential books in the founding of the United States of America. Rutherford's careful refutation of the divine rights of kings released the inevitable fission material that would change the face and future of nations forever. Once the energy of the sun was unleashed it could never be put back in the bottle again. In this sense *Lex, Rex* is a book that contains the ideas of Prometheus, harnessing the power of an energy of the cosmos. Indeed, the molecular structure of nation-states began to change because of the ideas in *Lex, Rex*. Rutherford's enumerated principles of governance could be resisted for a season — even from 1917 until 1989 — but the ideals set forth by the Scottish minister and professor at St. Andrews were imputed into the very DNA of Western democracy.

Today, the energy of this extraordinary book is as potent as it was when Rutherford wrote it. But the conditions in the Western democracies — constitutional monarchies and the Democratic Republics alike — are no doubt weakening. To be sure, it is not the ideas of *Lex, Rex* that are withering, but the unwise casting off of that truth which remains ever virulent to subdue autocrats, Socialists, and Communists.

What one learns is that the supposed and ruthlessly assumed divine right of kings to usurp the rule of law was but a symptom of humankind's fallen condition. Today, nearly 375 years after the publication of Samuel Rutherford's classic catechism on freedom, neo-fascists, anarchists, tyrannical despots, and mindless, reality-ignoring "politically correct" police, typically on guard in the classrooms of our oldest and most prestigious universities, threaten the mind, and thereby the God-given liberty, of an entire generation. Political and societal incarceration behind the infamous, dark iron bars of lies — and a foolish denial of the liberty that comes from Jesus Christ and his gospel — brings about much more than cultural phenomena. Such incarceration limits the human spirit. When the image of God is cloaked in the darkness of willful self-deception, the dark demons of falsehood come out of the walls like the "Clay Men" in Flash Gordon.

Is there still a fire in this book? If there is not, the book was never true. But it there is, and it was. The release of *Lex, Rex* with annotations – a book that explores the principles of freedom and the ultimate authority of God's word – is as relevant as ever. To continue the metaphor used earlier, it is as hot as ever. And emerging democracies in the global South, the global East, and the sprawling urban areas of even the Mideast, behind women in cloth prisons whose burqas move fearfully through state-controlled markets, are not the only likely new beneficiaries of Rev. Rutherford's magnus opus. No, the freedom-forged Western democracies, poisoned by the promises of Enlightenment lies, are desperately dying for an antidote.

Here we must admit that the question is not, "Is there a clearly discernible biblical truth of how Man shall govern himself?" That answer was surely enshrined in the legacies, laws, constitutions, and covenants of British, Commonwealth, European, and North American nations. The answer to such an essential question, though sadly shrouded in the ghostly veil of popular ignorance, remains embedded in the cornerstone of Western Civilization. Yes, God has revealed the necessity of human government, drawn its limits, defined its purpose, delineated its powers, and demanded both obedience rendered and honor shown to legitimate government. He has shown us what tyranny is and why the unholy beast must be opposed.

The question is also not, "How must civil government rightly relate to God?" Critical matter has also been sought and discovered, studied and concluded, codified and qualified by the most brilliant political and philosophical lights in our Western democracies. Though the European Union notoriously rejected the Judeo-Christian traditions of the member states it claimed to represent, codifying a supposed liberation from God and government, it remains to be seen if that glaring omission will become the fissure that destroys their novel experiment. Equally important is the necessary question, "How should the Church of our Lord Jesus Christ properly relate to the civil magistrate?" Once more, the carefully-thought-out answer to this question has already been considered and embraced with glorious restoration. National responses to the question exist on a settled continuum: from the Erastian framework of that famous benevolent Empire where the sun never set, to the careful Constitutional protection of all religions by her prodigious New World daughter. We contend that though the moral foundation of human government may be buried beneath the ruin and ruble of irresponsible neglect and intentional sabotage, when unearthed the treasure chest of Rutherford's royal expositions and the golden beams of liberty will shine as brightly as ever before. The question is not, "Can the fire of freedom burn?" but rather, "Can it burn again?"

I believe I know the answer as surely as I know the question: "With the truth of God that saves there is also renewal of the human soul." And these principles of freedom will ignite and cast their warm golden glow over even the darkest corners of stifling Statism. The light of God's word that guides governments into "sunlit uplands" of divinely bestowed freedom can forever be trusted to accomplish all that God has intended. And when that light is aglow, people are not only freed, human souls are healed. It is for this reason then, that this new edition of Samuel Rutherford's *Lex, Rex* is now unleashed again. May God use the late Prof. Rutherford's catechism in liberty, and the humble annotations thereunto attached, to stir the hearts of men and women all over the world to reach out and take this lantern of liberty for themselves. To those yet in the darkness of tyrannical rule, whether spiritual, physical, or civil, I say to you, "And ye shall know the truth, and the truth shall make you free" (John 8:32).

To my fellow pilgrims in the winnowing, winding days of this twenty-first century I say to you: Awaken! Let us throw off the heavy shackles forged by biblical illiteracy—it is within our power if we will but repent and believe— and let us return to the Truth that the Law — the revealed Word of the living God, the incorruptible Law of the Lord, as well as the irreducible Law of the image of God stamped upon our souls, "eternity in our hearts" (Ecclesiastes 3:11)—is truly and really our lauded sovereign. Thus, this is not a title, but rather a cry: LEX, REX!

May this book in some way help to advance what St. Paul admonished to those who had possessed the treasure of self-government, the blessings of representative governance, and the undiminished good of a civil government that is accountable to the People that allowed its existence; and to the God who requires righteousness and benevolence in rulers:

"Stand fast therefore in the liberty wherewith Christ hath made us free and be not entangled again with the yoke of bondage" (Galatians: 5: 1).

M.A.M.

Introduction

To research, write, and read *Lex, Rex* (translated "the Law is King," or "The King and the Law") by the Reverend Samuel Rutherford is a considerable undertaking. It is, indeed, an investment of time, intellectual capital, and all of this enforced by physical energy. It is not so much that the material is a massive tome, like War and Peace, but rather that Rutherford's masterpiece requires theological reflection, practical observation, and critical thinking, i.e., building the bridge from theological concepts to practical application. In order to make such a substantial investment it seems to me that there must be at least three questions that should be answered.

The first question is this, "Has the volume contributed to the intellectual and theoretical construction of modern democracies?"

I am asking the question, "Is it worth my time to read?" Answering that question is a resolute "yes." It is not so much that Benjamin Franklin and Thomas Jefferson held their copies of *Lex, Rex* as they penned the founding documents of the United States of America, but rather that by the time of the codification of America's independence, the mind of Rutherford was already well-established in the body politic on these shores. We do not have to use a digital search engine to see if Rutherford or *Lex, Rex* ever appear in any of the salient constitutional documents (for instance, *Lex, Rex* is not in the Federalist papers). We merely have to see that the grandfathers of the founding fathers were well-versed in Samuel Rutherford's great work and indeed quoted it prolifically. Witherspoon, for instance, was schooled in Edinburgh. He taught at Princeton. One of his students was James Madison. There is no doubt whatsoever that Witherspoon, the only clergyman to sign the Declaration of Independence, consumed Rutherford's principles of governance. It is equally implausible that Madison could sit at the feet of Witherspoon without imbibing the mind of Rutherford. He also was taught the secularized interpretation of Rutherford through the work of John Locke. Look at the principles appealed to for resistance to Great Britain (or more, specifically, to the Court of King George III). You will observe the arguments not unlike those used to oppose the Jacobite intrusions into the Magna Carta rights of English citizens. Tyranny had to be resisted, peacefully, through appeals, but, then, if there is no redress, Rutherford would say, the body seeking remedy from the oppressive power may either flee or fight. Clearly, unequivocally, Rutherford was present in the Pennsylvania State House (later, Independence Hall) by his unprecedented influence on the reasoning of those gathered. But there is more.

The founding documents of our nation go far past the Constitution, the Declaration of Independence, and those several famous manuscripts which supported independence, like the influential Federalist Papers. The founding documents must include the sermons of the great Presbyterian, Congregational, Baptist, Anglican, and other ministers of the gospel in New England and on the Atlantic colonial coast. So, yes, Samuel Rutherford's *Lex, Rex* was extraordinarily influential in the founding of this nation. *Lex, Rex*, like the Westminster Confession of Faith, like Scottish philosophical concepts, like English law, and like English-speaking and Dutch spirituality, all converged — yes, and crashed, with other philosophies, most predominantly that of the French Revolution and Enlightenment — as part of the compendium of thinking that, at length, led to John Hancock's signature. To study constitutional law, to study early American history, to consider the theological development of the Church in North America, or to study public policy or public administration, one would certainly desire a functioning familiarity with "Rutherford's rights." You can of course go without it but your understanding of the pillars of modern democracy will be diluted. The strong pillars will stand, even if the *Lex, Rex*-challenged observer is not exactly sure how the pillars stand. This book is written that you may know the ingredients of a modern moral democracy, the pillars of benevolent government for the people and by the people.

I pause to address the phrase, "modern moral democracy." I have deliberately selected these words to make the phrase because I wanted to describe something unseen but quite real that lies beyond a mere functional democracy, that is representative government, whether in Constitutional Monarchy (e.g., Great Britain) or Republicanism (the United States of America). A "moral democracy" is one in which the rudiments of the system are so critical to its continual existence that they must be forever codified in its name, its description. Ours is a "moral democracy" in that the morals, the guiding principles of self-governance, are manifestly evident in our articles of confederation. Quite simply, we are bound to each other and to "Nature's God" by the morals He has laid down in His Word, the Holy Bible. This is quite different from the European Union's secularist constitution, which seeks to codify the foundations of their democratic idea without God. Shall such a system stand? It seems highly unlikely since it either opposes or merely dismisses the oxygen that gives life to both self-governance, consent of the governed, and a divine vision of inalienable rights.

Back to my main point. I believe that one should read this, study this, consider this, and make the investment of time and energy, because the document is an extraordinary and seminal force in the formation of the United States of America. Moreover, if you're reading this from Great Britain or from any of the British Commonwealth countries, or if you're reading this from Russia, China, Iran, North Korea, or a host of other nations without the benefit of English law and Judeo-Christian theological foundations of this system of government, then you have before you a remarkable document that can renew or establish a God-ordained government in your land. Indeed, the concepts articulated in this remarkable manuscript are nothing more or less than the very mind of Almighty God as his Word is revealed to us through his son Jesus Christ. Rutherford has studied and distilled the mind of God revealed in Scripture and articulated, defended, and advanced those holy principles of human governance that give birth to human liberty, liberty of conscience, and liberty of the spirit. You have before you the very documents which could bring your own governments renewal or, as it was in the American colonies, a necessity to reestablish the principles of governance that have been part of our own history in the English-speaking world.

Another question that we have is this: "is it relevant?" In other words, am I holding in my hand a splendid record that not only had a tremendous impact upon the founding of the nation, but has (and can have) a continuing constructive consequence in our lives today? That is a fair question. It is more than a fair question; it is an unquestionably essential question. We do not have time for mere academic inquiry in today's world. We must have academic inquiry which will give birth to practical solutions. Samuel Rutherford's *Lex, Rex* is just that. And for you and me to take the time to research and study its claims is to invest in contemplations about principles — Rutherford and no less than Burke, Madison, Jefferson, Lincoln, Churchill, and Reagan would all say principles that are timeless, irreducible, and irrefutable — that can make a difference today.

Lex, Rex is a formidable sack of seeds. The seeds have proleptic power that if harnessed in our own day will produce a stunning harvest of new freedom. I believe that I should warn you that upon studying the kernel of *Lex, Rex* you will no doubt observe that this seed has an incredible antivirus coating. The antiviral agency is built-in to the very molecular make-up of each seed of truth. Thus, intrusive governments, elitism, fascism, socialism, communism, capitalism without compassion, and any concept in which government is independent of the consent of the governed and their God-given rights to liberty, are identifiable enemies of *Lex, Rex*. The antiviral powers within the seeds of truth will immediately attack and dismantle the harmful viruses. And we must say that we see such virulent madness in our own day. We see such viruses taking away the crop of liberty in many fields. We see the intrusion of government in every area of life, but beyond that, we see the viral pandemic of a government without God and, consequently, without God-given liberties being recognized. Only look around. There appears to be an increase of wholly tolerated, if not endorsed, fascism on the campuses of some of our great universities. Like any malicious virus, the warring agent of truth begins to dismantle all vestiges of the older ideas. The ideas are preserved within the sacred coating. The seeds remain.

But the golden-grain fields of good which sprout from the seeds of *Lex, Rex*-thinking are subject to the viral ideas of godless tyranny. Thus, the culture – the accumulation of laws, religion, institutions, economics, the arts and sciences, all products of the truth that burst open and grew from the seed – is subject to viral infection and unavoidable destruction. Free men and women, freethinking men and women, must be vigilant. And when you are told to "sit down and be quiet," be aware that the virus is rampant.

But the nature of the virus is subtle. It conceals itself inside of carrier-agents like intellectualism (pseudo), globalism, multi-culturalism, and that most damning of conditions, unreasoned and impulsive "utilitarianism." The response to such autocratic stifling of the vox popli (the voice of the people) – and, invariably, suppression of vox Domini (the voice of the Lord) – is, of course, that the ideas of *Lex, Rex* are, in fact, quite portable, around the globe. The ideas transcend native customs and traditions. The principles of *Lex, Rex* are unquestionably practical. Yet, the triad of globalism, multi-culturalism, and utilitarianism, in our case, is an unholy trinity fashioned as a rhetorical weapon to destroy their enemies, or a scythe, to cut down the green-garden of liberty. The fashionable confederacy of ideas will forever reject God and His truth at any expense, but their own. In that event the opponents of moral democracy are both traitors to the God-implanted truth in their hearts and cowards. For, "Also, he has put eternity into man's heart . . ."

Christianity, as Samuel Rutherford demonstrates, is no friend of absolutism. Christianity stands on its own principles, its own truth claims, and invites—if not dares—others to stand with it. We asked the question, "Are the claims of Jesus Christ beneficial for your life? Is the presence of the Church a blessing or curse? Do you find that you have more blessings from this other religion than you do from the faith of our Lord Jesus Christ? Has Christianity served the "common good?" Then go there! If Christ is not Christ, if he is not raised from the dead, then we of all men or most to be pitied!" Remember Elijah's challenge?

"And Elijah came near to all the people and said, 'How long will you go limping between two different opinions? If the LORD is God, follow him; but if Baal, then follow him.' And the people did not answer him a word" (1 Kings 18:21).

They did not answer because they can never answer. The answer is self-indicting. The God of Abraham, Isaac, and Jacob, the God of St. Paul and St. Peter and of Augustine, is unafraid of the text. Thus, Christianity stands with the other great religions of the world and says, "The ground on which we stand is level. We demand that all religions and all men who hold to their ideas can stand upon this ground and have their say. Then, let us respond. Then, let evidence and truth have its way." Yet, the spirit of "cooperation without compromise," as we referred to it when I was an Army Chaplain, is a spirit on decline. What to do? Rutherford's *Lex, Rex* is an antidote to this pandemic of what philosopher Charles Taylor called "objectification and excarnation"—the removal of the Imago Dei, leaving man without Incarnation, and, so, viewing human beings as a commodity. So, absolutely, it should be picked up and read and studied and distributed. It is relevant for the University. It is relevant for the galleries and chambers of government, here in the United States, Canada, Great Britain, the great Commonwealth nations, Western Europe, the Middle East, as well as the emerging giants of the Pacific. And I must say that if the truths contained in *Lex, Rex* are, indeed, of divine origin, they are good not only for families of nations but for families, that most holy and seminal component in society. I would pray that heads of households would ensure that the principles of *Lex, Rex* were placed into the minds of their children, beginning at a very young age. Oh, may the children of this generation mature with a deep and rich biblical conviction of the God-given rights of human beings to be self-governed. Place the potent seed of *Lex, Rex* into the heart and mind of a child and he will inevitably burst forth as a champion for self-government and lover of liberty.

Yes, the seed of *Lex, Rex* is a powerful spore that can withstand viral attack even as it establishes a field of freedom and over-flowing silos of liberty that can feed generation after generation. There is no limit to its power. Like all inalienable rights, the doctrines of *Lex, Rex* are preserved. They may be attacked. They cannot be destroyed. Yet, the fields of good which they produce are continually attacked by the malevolent forces that oppose God and His truth. History is the witness to the horrid reality that the fruit of inalienable rights can and are frequently assaulted and obliterated. Yet, the seed remains for another generation to plant again. The seeds of inalienable rights are impervious to the whims of madmen and the inhuman mechanizations of deep-state autocracies. Read Rutherford. Discover the seed. Plant the seed. It will always grow, even over the ravaged and burned-over fields of despots or inattentive citizenry. In fact, the seeds of liberty often grow at a greater rate in the blackened fields of licentiousness or totalitarianism. The cry of the human heart is more distinct having been, at one time, suppressed.

The last question that we might have is this, "Is it reasonable?"

Samuel Rutherford was a man of his age. To be quite clear, he was an especially skilled theologian in an age of noteworthy theologians. The Reverend Samuel Rutherford was an extraordinary expositor in an age of prodigious preachers. He was a consummate biblical shepherd in an era when Almighty God blessed the English-speaking world with many such dedicated pastors. If the English language is considered to have been at its apex in the Elizabethan Age, when crowds of common Londoners listened to the sermons of John Donne (1572-1631), which confound us with its "conceits" and soaring metaphoric expressions of Biblical truth, this language, by the 1640s and the 1650s, was yet a language of considerable capacities for both grammatical precision and duteous portrayal. The modern reader, however, might find that some of the notions of Rutherford are hidden behind a curtain of an inaccessible idiom and quite possibly a hard-to-follow logic. Thus, the publisher has undertaken to employ me in this groundwork of writing annotations for each of the 44 questions and answers within *Lex, Rex*. So, the very question that you might ask, "Is it readable? Is it understandable?" This is the very reason for this book.

As to whether we succeed to making the volume accessible will be judged by the reader. For it remains now only to ask God's blessings upon this volume, to pray ardently that the Lord will bring a fresh clarity to the biblical principles that Rev. Rutherford so diligently and faithfully mined, and that in my own work, I may be faithful to say what Rutherford said, and just say it in a way that reaches the minds of today's professors, students, pastors, churchmen, citizens of all types, and men and women all over the world who desire the kind of human government that God intended and that Rutherford unveils.

Now unto him who can do these things and more, we give all honor and glory and all praise. And we trust that when we have done our best to proclaim the unsearchable riches of Christ and the mind of God concerning human government and the human spirit that people will not only live free in this life, but come to embrace the One who has granted these precious and inalienable rights and live free forever.

In the name of the Father, and of the Son, and of the Holy Spirit. Amen.

M.A.M.

Rutherford and the Providence of God

A BIOGRAPHICAL REFLECTION

"The lines of life are never long when seen from and to end." How poetically accurate. And yet, what remarkable events may occur in the brief distance of such lines! There is no more remarkable instance of this truth than in the life of Samuel Rutherford (1600-1661).

Several insightful and thorough biographies have been offered of Rutherford. The Dictionary of National Biography (DNB), 1885-1900, Volume 50, provides one of the more thorough and interesting biographical sketches of the great seventeenth-century Scottish reformer. The author of that entry is an interesting subject in his own right, the Rev. Dr. George Washington Sprott. Dr. Sprott served in several capacities, including Professor, missionary, and minister of the gospel

Samuel Rutherford was born in 1600 in the parish of Nisbet in the county of Roxburgh about 4 miles from the town of Jedburgh which is just inside the boundary of Scotland in what is now called the Borders Region of Scotland.

An Engraving of Edinburgh University

In 1617 he went to the University of Edinburgh, where he studied classics, philosophy and physics for 4 years. He graduated with a Master of Arts Degree, and 2 years later in 1623 he was appointed the Professor of Latin language and Literature at the University, and was called the Regent of Humanities.

in several parishes. Originally from Nova Scotia, George Washington Sprott became known, for most, for his scholarly contributions to Reformed liturgics and to the proposed union of the several schismatic branches within the Church of Scotland. For our own purposes, Sprott provides a biography that is both scholarly and attentive; attentive to the essential character, devout Christian faith, and stalwart application of that character and faith of Samuel Rutherford. This life sketch shall in no way compete with such a fine scholarly contribution. We have retained his legacy to us in Appendix C. However, the aim of this little biographical sketch is to investigate, isolate, and seek the glory of God in those several critical Providential "turns" in the forward movement of this extraordinary life. Specifically, I want to ask the questions, "What are the salient events and features of life necessarily assembled (as only God can do)? And how do these isolated events converge to form a man such as Samuel Rutherford, a man for his times if ever there was one, and yet a man whose prophetic lines of thought extend through the centuries into our own day?"

The first feature in the life of Samuel Rutherford must surely be his name, and by "his name" I mean to say the heritage of Rutherford. For the man who would rise to defend the God-given rights of liberty and to call kings to account was not a McDonald or a Stewart or a Robertson, but a name whose etymological origins undoubtedly lie in the very geographical area of his birth. The surname "Rutherford" is of old middle English origins. Rutherford is a place name. The "ford" part of the name is quite clear. Ford is referring to the English word for the crossing of a river or a small body of water. The first part of the name has some mystery in it. It may very well be, as some have supposed, a "cattle crossing." Thus, his forbearers might have been border country (where Rutherford was, indeed, born).

This leads to a second feature: the geography of Rutherford. Samuel Rutherford was born in village of Nisbet, near Jedburgh in the Scottish Borders area of Scotland. These Rutherfords might have once been cattlemen who were singularly known for a settlement near one of the many fords situated on the English-Scottish border. Now, I mentioned these particular points of interest – name and geography

When Rutherford completed his theological studies in 1627 he responded to an invitation from Sir John Gordon of Lochinvar to come to pastor the church in the parish of Anwoth in Galloway, and Rutherford was to be its first pastor.

In 1634, Rutherford's work came to the attention of the Bishop of Brechin, an ardent Arminian, and Rutherford was charged with nonconformity and with treason against the King. He was found guilty and began a period of exile. For the next 22 months, he was to live in a room at No. 44 Upper Kirkgate, in Aberdeen, away from home and friends, forbidden to preach in public by his enemies.

– because the man who would stand before the nation in one of the most dire and uncertain periods of Great Britain's history, espousing the Gospel of Jesus Christ as a truth that would set men free, even shaping human government in his own country and far beyond, was a man whose sympathies could not be chalked up as merely "assumed Pictish rebelliousness," (if such a calumny is supported). What I'm saying is that this is no local prince of the Highlands who "needs" to show up an English monarch. To the contrary, Samuel Rutherford must be recalled as a most irenic spirit whose very name and family history tie him to that border country of England and Scotland where the mountainous hatred is diluted into the larger, cold-water streams that give life to the land and to the People, the Lowland Scots and the Cumbrians alike. This seems a fitting site for a man named Rutherford.

The surname, Rutherford, and his place of birth in the village of Nisbet, doesn't necessarily evidence that a family of the Low Scots, that while not entirely free from skirmishes with the Cumbrian peoples of England, were more suitable to produce a man who would speak for all of the British people in a time when such a man was needed. However, these features did not exist in isolation. They became providential building blocks that produced the spiritual DNA that produced Rutherford and his ideas. For another strand of divine guidance is evident in timing.

The Lord chose to bring Samuel Rutherford into the world in (likely) the same year as the second son of James VI of Scotland and Anne of Denmark, Charles I (1600-1649). Born in Fife, Scotland, less than 120 miles from Rutherford's Nisbet, the Duke of Albany, as he became known at his baptism, would become the fuse that would ignite a nation over the idea of the rule of law. Though he was the son of Scottish royalty, Charles I inherited the throne of England and Scotland (after his brother Henry died of typhoid fever, in 1625) and proved to be a disastrous king for both countries in the Realm. The timing connection between Rutherford and Charles I extends beyond their birth year. It goes to the spirit of the times. Charles I and Samuel Rutherford were both born in Scotland, both in 1600, only miles apart. But their lives could not be further apart on the great issues of their time. Indeed,

Anwoth Church Today

Rutherford left Aberdeen of his own accord during 1638, Some think that he was present in Edinburgh for the signing of the National Covenant on March 1st. Other writers report that Rutherford, apparently back in Anwoth, hurried to Edinburgh and was one of the first to sign. Paintings of the scene do show him at the signing.

St. Mary's College in St. Andrews

Rutherford's gifts could no longer be confined to a small parish in Galloway. The General assembly of the Church of Scotland suggested that he be appointed the Professor of Divinity at St Mary's College in St Andrews.

Charles I married a French Catholic princess, Henrietta Maria (1609-1669), who refused to take part in Protestant worship. Elizabeth I (1533-1603), who preceded Charles' father, famously constructed a "middle way" for Anglicanism. This brought at least a superficial covering to the anger beneath the waterline of public faith. Under Charles, the crimson angst that led to Elizabeth's "Via Media," like an undigested piece of rotted beef, was not only regurgitated, but spit out, at each other. Much of this was due to the King's relationship with the equally disastrous Archbishop William Laud (1573-1645). Laud, a political figure who saw the doctrine of the divine right of kings as the necessary pattern for a divine right of bishops, successfully urged the King to take a decidedly Anglo-Catholic-anti-Calvinist position in his practice of Christianity. In following the unwise advice of his Archbishop, Charles I became, in several ways, a veritable caricature of the despotic, removed monarch who seemed to thrive on the concept which Rutherford (and so many of the young gentry of the Realm, the English Puritans) opposed. Thus, two men, Samuel Rutherford and Charles I, born in the same year and in the same region of the nation, yet worlds apart in their family backgrounds, would intersect on history's tattered pages as emblematic figures in a violent debate over an idea. One man would become a prisoner of his own royalty, on the Isle of Man, and ultimately lose his head at Whitehall in London. The other man would become royalty, as well. Rutherford was a royal ambassador for King Jesus. But he, too, would lose his freedom. In prison in Aberdeen, Rutherford demonstrated grace in winter. The pastor-scholar composed some of the most touching pastoral epistles to parishioners since the days of St. Paul.

In 1661, after the Restoration of the Monarchy by Charles II, Samuel Rutherford was summoned to be tried for treason. The reason? The book you are about to study was deemed a threat to the monarchy. In truth, it was a friend. The ideas of Rutherford do not destroy kings but allow them to reign within a constitution of freedom and fairness, which, in turn, promotes an active and happy citizenry. The author of Lex, Rex, the great Scottish Divine of the Westminster Assembly, did not appear. But he did respond, "Tell them that I have got a summons already from a Superior Judge and judicatory, and I behove [must] answer my first

Jerusalem Chamber – Westminster Abbey

Rutherford was one of the Church commissioners sent to London by the Scottish church. Rutherford moved to London, and stayed from November 1643 to November 1647. Besides the work spent on preparing the Westminster Confession of Faith, he was one of the main contributors to the Larger and Shorter Catechism in October 1647.

In 1644 he wrote his most famous and controversial book entitled "Lex, Rex", or the "The Law and the Prince" and next to his "letters" this is one of his achievements for which he is best remembered. This book was not just a spiritual treatise on the subject of the Church and the State, but it has been noted as one of the most valuable contributions to political science ever written. Many of the principles here soon found their way into the constitution of countries around the world.

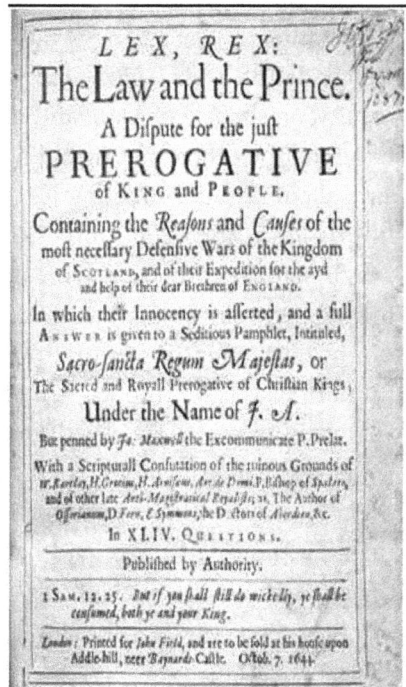

summons; and ere [before] your day arrives, I will be where few kings and great folks come."

Samuel Rutherford died on 30 March 1661.

The final strand of divine providence that shaped this man was the free choice of God in choosing Rutherford to become His son, by faith in God's Son, Jesus Christ. Samuel Rutherford saw the liberty of the human soul as a divine right of all men. This transformed sinner who would become a champion of grace, believed that the Levitical law of the Old Testament was fulfilled in Jesus Christ. The Theocratic law of Moses was completed when Israel became a monarchy. But he argued from Scripture that the moral Law of God has never ceased. We are a people under the Law: the law of love to drive us to see ourselves as needing a Savior; the law of love that guards our families and civic lives together; and the law of love that shapes our decisions, our priorities, and our motivations. Rutherford held no tension between Law and Love. Rutherford believed that we follow law, the "eternity in our hearts" as well as the Ten Commandments, as a forgiven sinner's duty of love to a gracious God, who sent His only begotten Son to keep that Law perfectly and become the sacrifice to pay the penalties of violating that Law.

Thus, Rutherford. And shall we not pray for such men and women to be formed in our own time? Against overwhelming "odds," confronted by civil war, a "world turned upside down," God used Samuel Rutherford to remind the world of this: "And you shall know the truth and the truth shall set you free."

"Oh, Lord God: Do it again."

M.A.M.

Samuel Rutherford died 29th March 1661.
He was buried in the churchyard at St. Andrews.

Rutherford lived to see all that he had striven for over thirty years crumbling before his eyes. An ideal church both in order and worship had been his vision, but the enemies of the gospel had ruthlessly trampled on all his achievements. Even with all these disappointments he never lost his zeal and love for his God and his Savior.

Acknowledgement

Pictures and Annotations courtesy Crich Baptist Church, Derbyshire, UK

On Samuel Rutherford and Lex, Rex

FRANCIS A. SCHAEFFER

He [Samuel Rutherford] has meant much to me for many years, but especially so from the time I began working on the material for the book and films How Should We Then Live? At that time I understood increasingly that Samuel Rutherford's Lex, Rex was an important trailmarker for our day. In the times I have spoken at St. Andrews University, the most outstanding thing for me was a feeling that Samuel Rutherford was not far away, that the old Rector was close by, and very contemporary!

In his classic work, Lex, Rex, Rutherford set forth the proper Christian response to nonbiblical acts by the state.

Rutherford argued that Romans 13 indicates that all power is from God and that government is ordained and instituted by God.

Acts of the state which contradicted God's Law were illegitimate and acts of tyranny.

Tyranny was defined as ruling without the sanction of God.

Rutherford held that a tyrannical government is always immoral.

He [Rutherford] said that 'a power ethical, politic, or moral, to oppress, is not from God, and is not a power, but a licentious deviation of power.'

It follows from Rutherford's thesis that citizens have a moral obligation to resist unjust and tyrannical government.

While we must always be subject to the office of the magistrate, we are not to be subject to the man in that office who commands that which is contrary to the Bible.

Taken from A Christian Manifesto by Francis A. Schaeffer, © 1981, Revised edition published in 1982, pp.5,6, 99-101. Used by permission of Crossway, a publishing ministry of Good News Publishers, Wheaton, IL 60187, www.crossway.org.

Editorial Notes

Dr. Samuel Rutherford posited and answered forty-four questions. The careful responses, together, form a polemical tome that advanced the Biblical ideals of liberty as a right for all mankind. The polemical form, however, is filled with otherwise obscure references, names, places, and events that would deserve their own annotations. The goal of this work is to make the ideas of *Lex, Rex* available to modern readers. Therefore, with the twin purposes of presenting *Lex, Rex* with readability and accessibility, the publisher presents:

1. The core matter of each question (in gray)
2. The centerpiece of Rutherford's answer (in gray)
3. The annotations by Dr. Milton

These central themes of Rutherford were isolated and selected for use in the respective chapters by the author. Therefore, rather than creating forty-four distinct chapters, we have created four major parts with eleven questions in each. We trust this will aid in your appreciation of this enormously influential work. *Lex, Rex* is a work that has influenced so much of modern democracy. If our editorial decisions work towards greater exposure of Rutherford's ideas, in secondary education and higher education, with clergy, with public officials, and in homes, then we will have considered the decision to be a successful one.

Rutherford's questions in the original are provided in Appendix B. There are a few questions that are specific to the contemporaneous places and events of Samuel Rutherford's seventeenth-century British Isles. In such cases, the author has restated Rutherford's questions, preserving the time-place reference, and then created a more universal question on the matter in brackets. Question 37 is an example of this editorial rule:

"Is it Biblically lawful for the powers of Scotland to defend their brethren, the protestants of England, against cavaliers? [Is it just for nations to rise in arms to defend other nations under siege of evil?]"

The goal of our editorial work is not merely to translate Rutherford into contemporary English, but to do so in a way that respects the historical landscape of seventeenth-century English civil and ecclesiastical conflict, while presenting the principial treasures of Rutherford's Biblical and logical thinking to people of all nations in our own day. We believe that the effect of this work is to unleash the light of Dr. Rutherford's brilliance and thus the light of Christ upon the matter of human government. Having done so, we have been amazed to see how relevant his work was to the Constitutional Monarchy of the United Kingdom and the Commonwealth of Nations, as well as to the founding Constitution of the United States of America. Rutherford has accomplished nothing less than identifying the captivity of human error and replaced it with the freedom of God, so carefully shown to be attested by the law written upon our hearts.

PART I

Lex, Rex
Questions 1-12

1

Is human government from God?

The power of government, in general, must be from God, because God reveals this in Romans 13:1; God calls for obedience to human governors in 1 Peter 2:13. I conclude, therefore, that all civil power is immediately from God for the good of Mankind.

Nothing is more fundamental in the study or consideration of mankind living in community than the God-given necessity of human government. Rutherford's first answer, being grounded in Romans 13, demonstrates that it is the will of God for man to live under governmental powers. We understand this first as children and when we recognize that our parents are our first governors. Our teachers, pastors, and Christian education leaders are also our governors. If we participate in other activities, such as Boy Scouts, or even a club, nothing is more essential than an immediate understanding of the need for government.

There are two things that are of concern to me in today's world about this fundamental gift of God: human government. First, we must remember that anarchy — the overthrowing of human government — is altogether sinful and un-biblical. More than that, because God made us we must say that it is unnatural. Therefore, those who in our own day seek to overthrow the temporal powers that have been given to us for a blessing do so at their peril. They not only are moving against natural law, but their fists are raised in disobedience and rebellion to God who gave us government. Secondly, we must be very careful that even when we have government that is not altogether to our liking we do not become like Israel and become murmurers. Rutherford rightly demonstrates that those who rule are, in fact, ministers of God. Therefore, we should pray for ministers. We should pray for those who govern us. If government is from God, and it most certainly is, then let us know we are all to support those governors; be they are parents, employers, teachers, law enforcement, or the political leadership that we elect.

2

Does natural law demonstrate government?

Natural Law demonstrates the reality of human government by prime example of the family. In family government, the head of the home, i.e., the father, has the power, like Adam, of both governing his family and defending his family against evil-doers. Also, we see the following:

1. *The powers that be, are of God (Rom. 13), therefore nature's light teaches that we should be subject to these powers.*
2. *It is against nature's light to resist the ordinance of God.*
3. *Let us not fear those who have been granted the "sword" for the terror of evil-doers.*
4. *Let us give honor to those who serve.*
5. *We must not withhold taxes due to the authorized human government.*

Rev. Rutherford rightly appeals to the family as the first order or the first appearance of human governance. It is here clearly demonstrated that the authority of the parents of the child were established by the very law of nature. We think of the passage from Ecclesiastes that God has put eternity in our hearts. Thus, governance is not only revealed by God in his word it is revealed in the very breast of mankind. Yet, it is also revealed that the abuse of such power, for example, a father abusing his child, is also a violent and wicked disregard for God and the law that he has placed into our hearts. To extrapolate this to the other spheres of governance leads us to not only defend that human government is good and revealed in the Word of God, but also that it is given to us by the light of nature. There is therefore a responsibility both by the governed and the governors. There is a responsibility of the child to show honor and deference and to pray for the parents. And the parent must be loving and careful to order his life so that he shelters and cares for the child. This is God's will for human governments. It is an awesome responsibility to be elected to office in human governments. I think it is well that we also say that to compare and contrast the different spheres or levels of governance is necessary to prevent us from becoming paternalistic. The role of the father is one of both authority and love. Government works best at all levels when those two vital components are present and actively pursued. There is a respect between the governed and the governor that brings honor and glory to God and brings peacefulness to humankind.

Western democracies are in peril whenever they lose the moral dimension and understanding of government. It is altogether true and undeniable that wickedness such as bribes, abuse of power, and "lording it over" the people, is due to fallen human nature. We must be all the more careful, then, to make sure that our ethical standards are such that we recognize this fallen nature and we guard against it. That being said, if we lose our ethical or moral ground for human governance, we risk losing our code. How very well I remember that Dr. D. James Kennedy was fond of saying, "When your creed cracks it is certain that your code will crumble."

3

Did God ordain certain kinds of human government, e.g., monarchy?

The forms of government (e.g., monarchy, constitutional monarchy, and republic) are not really different in specie and nature. Every form is from God. However, specific governments are ordinances of men. We obey lawful (and not tyrannical) governors, according to the Fifth Commandment, and in doing so, obey God.

It is of great interest to note that Samuel Rutherford, before establishing the divine rule of the consent of the governed, must do battle with anarchists and radicals who suppose that the king (and we may say in our own day, a constitutional monarchy as well as a Republic) cannot be from God. In fact, Rutherford draws from both the old and the new Testaments to demonstrate that the king rules best when he is ruling to the King of kings and Lord of lords. He is appointed as God's minister.

One of the great challenges in the seventeenth-century was the collapse of the Puritan middle. By using the term "the Puritan middle," I mean to say that wise, thoughtful, broad spirited group of men, of which Samuel Rutherford was an excellent model, had to endure the ill-advised, unbiblical, and, ultimately self-defeating, foolish activities of Puritan radicals from the left such as the fifth monarchist movement.

We should learn from the events of seventeenth-century England, Wales, Scotland, and Ireland, that we advance the kingdom of God best when we defend the rights of governors. When governors do err, as even officers in the church do, we may exercise duly appropriated avenues for redress; but we should also, all the more, seek to pray for those who are our superiors in human governance. As the writer to the Hebrews says, it is self-condemning when we fail to pray in support of our pastors and elders and other church leaders. In a similar way, we do hurt ourselves when we seek opportunities to stand against the government rather than to support it with our prayers and our encouragements. We must remember that the cause of Christ advances whenever there is peacefulness. Yes, it advances whenever there is tyrannical government as well. But it does so at the cost of blood and great treasure. It is better to seek the peace and purity of the power over us so that it may go better for ourselves. This is not only to the glory of God but to the good of humankind.

4

Is the King's office only by allowance of God or do the People have a part to play?

The king is from God. The king is also from the People. Government is a human ordinance (1 Peter 2:3). So, People create the king. To look to David as a norm for human government is not right. For David was anointed by God. We do not order the norm by the extraordinary.

Rutherford begins to strike a very important note in the fourth question. Would the unjust authorities seize the great Reformer before he could complete this monumental work? But Rutherford does make the turn. He does begin to demonstrate from the Word of God that a king or any governor of the people is not only appointed through the providence of God but that Providence is mediated through the approbation of the people. Therefore, the divine right of kings is rejected. The right of the kingdom rule is given from God and is recognized by the people. The consent of the governed was an extraordinarily important principle that Edmund Burke received from Rutherford and passed on to our founding fathers. More than that, this great truth was embedded in the New England pilgrims and the Jamestown English settlers. There is a natural desire in the heart of a child to please his parents. He desires to show his love and affection for them. Why? Because the parents love the child. The parents protect the child. Even when the parents are forced to discipline, the child will, ultimately, recognize that the discipline is that of caution, love, and desire to prevent something terrible from happening to the child. And so I ask you who are parents:

you believe that you have inalienable parental rights and your position as a father or mother is granted by God, but do you not also recognize the need of the child?

How many times in my pastoral career have I seen these truths, so brilliantly exposited by Samuel Rutherford, disregarded by pastors and elders and other leaders in the church. Believing that their call has granted them a certain right of governance they forget that that goal was mediated through the people. Their relationship as a "father" to the congregation is just that: a relationship. It is not a tetherless authority, a ruthless right to rule without regard to the blessings which are due to the people. Rutherford's answer to the question as to whether the king is from God only or also from men is answered very wisely. When we see a leader elected, the king crowned, a prime minister taking his place with the ruling party in a parliament, we must remember that God himself has been working through the people. Unless it can be demonstrated that governing power has become tyrannical and therefore no godly power at all, then we are required to pray for kings and all who are in authority. They are from God through the people. And we should remember this in every sphere of governance, including the local church, the school, employment, organizations, and, that first and most precious government, the family.

5

Are Kings and other rulers ordained "immediately" (i.e., "directly") by God or given the authority to rule "mediately" (by "means" or "secondary causes") by the governed?

The concept of authority in governance is truly from God. However, God has ordained the means as well as the end. The Scriptures demonstrate how People make a king. Thus, the office is from God, but the approbation of a human to that office is granted unto the People.

We must recall that as this document has the distinct roma of polemic, it is, in fact, an answer to a very forceful assertion by "Erastians, Anabaptists, Independents, and other sectaries" of the time. The object of Rutherford's retort had written, "The king is no creature of the people's making." This strikes at the very core of Rutherford's understanding of the Word of God. He acknowledges the sovereignty of God in dealing with mankind, including providentially placing rulers over the nations of the earth (and the churches of the land). Yet, an appeal to Moses or to David does not prove a royal absolutist position. Certainly, God was sovereign in the appointment of Moses and David, yet there was, indeed, an approbation of God's people. The matter of the apostle Matthias, elected by the divine casting of lots in the book of acts is taken as a pretense, once more, for absolute sovereignty. Yet, Rutherford wisely and correctly demonstrates that it was the other disciples who mutually recognized the method in which they would seek the will of God in the matter. Rutherford's thinking is brilliant at this point. It is brilliant and yet it is simple; not simpleminded, but plain. God is sovereign. Yet he manifests his sovereignty through his people.

This would become an extraordinary principle in the moral democracies that would emerge. Edmund Burke would popularize Rutherford's thinking in his defense of the American colonies in the stamp act. Burke believed that the people who have been governed had the right, if they were going to be taxed, even penalized, to participate or be represented in their own governments. No one denied the right of King George III to be king. What was denied was an absolutism which disregarded the representation of the people and the consent of the governed.

Rutherford's teaching is important on many levels at once in today's world. We must remember that God does indeed appoint rulers. It is God, for instance, who calls ministers to proclaim the unsearchable riches of Christ. Yet no man takes this honor to himself, writes the author to the Hebrews. Absolutism, despotism, and a lone-wolf approach to ordination is thereby biblically forbidden. Though God calls a man to preach it will take a judicatory of the church to recognize that call and, of course, a local parish of that judicatory to issue the call. Thus, once more, we see how sovereignty is mediated through the representation of the people.

It is important to see, on the other hand, that Rutherford in no place denies the ruling prerogatives of a king in a biblically constitued moral government (who rules by allowance of the People). He just believes that the king is not above the law. There can be no absolutism and no appeal to God's sovereignty in order to establish an absolute sovereignty of a ruler. No. The ruler is sovereignly chosen by God through the people. Having said that, it is vital to recognize that it is, indeed, an act of God's sovereignty. What is needed today is both humility on the side of statesmen, public officials, royalty, prelates, church officials, and employers, as well as those who have consented to their governments as being of natural law, and, therefore, a good and necessary entity that deserves appropriate submission. An equal dose of humility and reliance upon the one true sovereign, the King of Kings, our Lord and Savior Jesus Christ, brings about a peaceable reasonableness that yields many blessings.

6

Is the office and role of the king or another governor merely acknowledged by the people or do they actually have a say in who governs them?

God governs all things. But shall we say that even pagan kings carry a direct anointing from God, as God ordained David? Of course not! Government is from God but is appropriated through the rights and the abilities He has given to the People.

Rutherford demonstrates through philosophical and theological moments that while God appoints sovereigns in human government, He does so through secondary means. He appeals to the Scriptures to demonstrate that God provides instructions to us on how to choose leaders, whether civil or ecclesiastical. If he is providing such guidance, then it follows that the Lord expects his people to fulfill his will according to his guidance. If the appointments of rulers were a direct act from God without human agency involved, there would be no need for instructions, no need for divine revelation and the Word of God concerning what constitutes godly leadership.

The difference between a democracy and a moral democracy is divine revelation guiding the citizenry as well as the elected representative leaders. Rutherford's political theory is altogether his theological conviction. Rutherford's design for government is drawn explicitly from Scripture. Yet, for Rutherford, natural law and divine law are, indeed, one and the same.

The challenge with democracies today may be this absence of a moral component. If we fancy that natural law is somehow divided from Almighty God, we lose the moral impulse in human government. To lose this moral component is to risk the unraveling of the rest of the Democratic government. For if human government is derived from God, not an abstract and unknowable natural law, but, in fact, a divine revelation, most fully revealed through the person of our God and Savior Jesus Christ, then such government and her people are subject to both blessings and penalties. The divine component which produces the moral impulse within a moral democracy safeguards against tyranny on the one hand and anarchy on the other.

7

Has it been demonstrated and proven that both the Constitution of human government and the ruler of a particular government are ordained by God and not allowed to rule by people?

God gives authority to those who rule "mediately" through the People, not "immediately" as He ordained Moses, David, and our Lord Jesus Christ. The People do not surrender their rights when they voluntarily allow a ruler to govern their communities. The king and the constitution are allowed by the People without any loss of individual rights.

Perhaps, the single most brilliant force of argument in *Lex, Rex* is demonstrated in question seven. The question concerns his opponents' assertions that neither Constitution nor king are established by the people. Samuel Rutherford uses Scripture, history (he masterfully goes to John Calvin to support his argument), and experience itself.

One of the things that is lost in a modern democracy in the West, at least, is the very brilliance we see demonstrated in this question: a lack of understanding concerning the moral dimensions of a democracy. We have in many ways lost our way from the Greco-Roman philosophical arguments for a moral democracy and have chosen to dispose of the priceless pearls of biblical truth and common sense that have come to us from those like Rutherford.

We would do well to study our Bibles and to move from theological reflection to critical thinking. Theological reflection focuses upon the text before us. We isolate the several linguistic, philosophical, existential, and historical variables within the text. We then reflect upon these in the context. We ask questions: what is the true meaning of this? What is its relationship to God's larger plan? How does this relate to the centrality of God's redeeming covenant in Jesus Christ? How does it relate to my life? How does this impact our community? What "common grace" is here to consider? And then we moved to applying the answers that we discover from the text in the context. We apply the divine truths to our lives and to our communities. This, then, is how we move from theological reflection to critical thinking. Samuel Rutherford demonstrates such a prodigious political velocity — indeed, one that gives the greatest and noblest models of liberty and human flourishing — because the great pastor — scholar of St. Andrews, first, knew his Bible. The gaps in his opponent's logic appear precisely because they are lacking in a coherent biblical theology and systematic theology.

8

Has anyone really demonstrated that the People are incapable of forming their own government?

No such proposition has been proven. The People by nature are equally indifferent to all the three governments (Monarchy, Aristocracy, Polity; the three-forms proposed by Aristotle; see notes below) and are not under any one by nature. To the contrary, nature and history show that the People are quite capable of forming their own government.

Aristotle proposed three-forms of government and six kinds of leaders. Consider this table:

Number of Rulers	Type	Perverted
Ruled by One	Monarchy	Tyranny
Ruled by a Few	Aristocracy	Oligarchy
Ruled by Many	Polity	Democracy*

* By "Democracy," Aristotle meant "mob rule." He saw this form of direct governance as one that would invariably degenerate. If Democracy is, indeed, the perverted form, then the Republic may be the preferred form. Likewise, in Monarchy, Tyranny is the perverted form. A Constitutional Monarchy (e.g., Great Britain) is the preference. This form of government was considered the best by Rutherford. The Commonwealth of England, realized under Cromwell, was a less preferred type of human governance according to Rutherford.

Aristotle's influence on Rutherford is pronounced. However, most view Aristotle's classification as limited. Alternatively, one may view it as genius in its simplicity. The other forms of government merely form from the three basic types.

9

If the power of a ruler is from the consent of the governed, cannot the governed resume self-governance in cases of tyranny?

The People have a God-given right to self-governance. God does not author tyranny. The natural law of self-defense cannot be taken away.

One of the central points in this part of Samuel Rutherford's thesis about the rule of law is the precious concept that every man and woman has inherent dignity and rights.

The reader will no doubt recognize that while one question builds upon the other, there is also the undeniable repetition of themes. I believe that this is without the need for apology. Rutherford arranged his thought in a literary device that is something akin to a musical "round" or canon perpetuus, in which the strict polyphonic theme remains the same and is carefully embellished to form a symphony of logic. This literary device builds like Pachelbel's Canon to overwhelm the reader (or rhetorical adversary) with irrefutable deductions. The result in *Lex, Rex* is not only a political philosophy that can ignite liberty in the most tyrannical place, but it is also a veritable affirmation of biblical faith. The result is that human beings are no longer commodities. Human beings are made in the image of God. Every human being is precious in the sight of God. And every human being has inalienable rights, granted by the Almighty, that prevent Royal overreach or unlawful governmental intrusion.

What will you and I do with this explication of the divine mind? How will we use the power that God has given us in this world? We have the right, and from the right flows the obligation, of self-governance and prayerful subordination to "God's ministers" who rule for the common good. But I see within this divine revelation a proleptic power that cannot only burst forth to new golden green field of liberty, but one that can result in such a human flourishing that generations upon generations are blessed. We do well to covenant with God and to plead with him to give us His blessing so that we may use these blessings to cultivate a Gospel landscape. For good government lays an even ground on which the gospel of Jesus Christ may go forward, not only in our generation, but until Christ comes again. This is the power that resides in one human being. This is the power, the divine right embedded within the image of God, that Rutherford defends, and we do well to follow.

10

In a monarchical government, is ruling power in the transmission of authority by birthright or does monarchy exist because the people allow it to exist?

Monarchy exists because the people allow it to exist. There is no inherent transmission of royalty between father and son. The disposition of rulership is allowed by the people. In the case of monarchical lineage, the people may allow such an aristocratic structure to exist. But it does not exist out of pure nature.

Rutherford did not oppose monarchy. Indeed, he will become a veritable thorn in the side of some English Puritans who deny monarchy and replace it, by regicide, with the short-lived Republican English Commonwealth. Dr. Rutherford prefers to make arguments at the point of representative government, which he sees as an inalienable right. Forms of government are not beneath debate, but they are secondary to the greater principle of government by whatever form must be by consent of the governed.

11

Is a King or ruler by right of descent more of a King than if elected by the People?

A king that is one by election more nearly accords with Scripture. If the People have the right to limit power of a ruler, so, too, do they have the natural right to allow power and royal descent.

No. A king has the power of governorship by the allowance of his subjects. Indeed, they may only be called "subjects" because they have acquiesced to be so. Whether through primogeniture or election, a ruler rightfully ascends to his position only through the uncompelled decision of a People.

12

May a kingdom be lawfully obtained by conquest through force of arms?

If conquest is by the consent of the People, then, "Yes, there is a lawful right to such a kingdom." But conquest, even lawfully, does not signify God's approval one way or the other. A bloody conqueror is not a blessing as a good king. We must remember that even a father cannot take away the rights of liberty of his children. Though he may govern them lawfully by God he cannot usurp God-given rights. So, too, a human government may rightfully make and uphold laws, but none can be made or upheld lawfully before God that usurps the rights of liberty given to every person at birth.

As far as Israel and David's conquests, these are promises of God in a theocracy or special dispensation of time. We do not order the norm of Scripture by the exception that God makes for certain key figures in Scripture.

The argument had been put forth that conquest itself makes for lawful kingship over the conquered peoples. Rutherford does not deny the biblical examples of Daniel and Jeremiah underneath the awful conquest of Nebuchadnezzar. God told the Jews to pray for the good of Babylon that it may go well with them also. However, Samuel Rutherford demonstrates that mere conquest by itself — the stronger over the weaker — cannot prove the legitimacy. Otherwise, the Amorites and other antagonists of ancient Israel would have the moral high ground in their victorious challenges to Israel. Rutherford shows that conquest that leads to consent is, indeed, a legitimate rule. Conquest that leads to tyranny is not sanctioned by God and must be resisted. What is most amazing about this particular enquiry is how Rutherford addresses the variables present in such an argument. Again, we witness the precise logical mind of this biblical scholar.

Can a moral democracy rest only upon brute strength - economic, military, or otherwise? Is strength itself a virtue of a great nation if such strength is deployed to oppress others? The answer is self-evident. It is also self-evident, then, that such a rule of the victorious party relates the answer to the question, "Will the conquerors be benevolent in the governance of the people?" Having subjugated the people, perhaps, because of God's judgment against a nation, does the conquering power harness its strength for the good and therefore legitimize its rule?

The global tensions that we face today can be viewed through a biblical lens. This is what Samuel Rutherford is teaching us. When one state invades another, and does so without provocation and without justifiable reasons, the conquering state is in danger of God's judgment. Indeed, it may be that God's judgment is meted out by the sense of indignity of the global community. Alternatively, when the state is weakened by its own sinfulness or even by the mysterious providences of circumstance and find it better for the people to be amalgamated into another nation, then there can be a biblically sanctioned new government. If only our leaders would read Rutherford, would read Edmund Burke, John Locke, and the framers of our own Constitution, they would arrive at better decisions concerning war and peace, conquest and liberation, and more easily secure the blessings of Almighty God. How we need such wisdom in our own day.

PART II

Lex, Rex
Questions 13-22

13

Does royalty and privilege to rule or govern come by birth or is it true that all men are born equal?

Royalty and privilege in any way in this life is not a seal of God's approval. Such governance does not come with birth (unless the People allow it to be so). Though Aristotle and Aquinas demonstrate that there are logical degrees of subjection in life, none of their arguments plead that it is a divine right. Every person is born under subjection to his parents, but that does not in any way repeal his God-given rights to liberty as a human being.

Nothing can summarize Samuel Rutherford's political philosophy any more than this simple sentence in this question: "Man by nature is under government paternal, not politic properly, but by the free consent of his will."

A moral democracy rests upon the great truth that all men are indeed created in the image of God and are born free. No one can deny that the circumstances of a fallen world may cast one into bondage. But the bondage is not inherent but imposed. Rutherford rightly agrees that the duty of gratitude and love to parent and spouse require good and godly subjection. Yet, he denies that a man has an intrinsic duty to subjection to political powers.

This question and the answers that Rutherford provides should in no way engender a libertarian mindset toward government. We remind ourselves of the lessons taught by both St. Paul and St. Peter: we are to be subject to all the governing authorities. Yet, when such governing authorities become tyrannical or in some other way unlawful, inhumane, or lacking in the consent of the governed, then we not only have a right to redress such a calamity, but a responsibility to do so. Alternatively, we must remember that Peter and Paul called for godly submission to the civil authorities connected to the Roman empire, with all the corruption and abuses that we now know existed. Yet, if a man is born or comes into such circumstances, as long as that government does not prohibit his conscience from expressing the laws of God, then he must prayerfully be bringing the names of the leaders unto God. It is for this reason that a man like Edmund Burke could support the American Revolution and yet decry the French Revolution. One was waged for the principles of a moral democracy and one was waged in violent opposition to legitimate authority. There is a way and means to secure a better government than beheading the monarch.

14

Is a king or ruler bound to his people by the right of covenant or by right of birth?

The King or any ruler is under a natural law of accountability and protection to the People. There is a covenant in the economy of God's sovereignty and will that ties a king and people together by the nature of the office of a governor. Rulers are ministers of God for the good of the People. However, the covenant is broken when the king or ruler takes undue power to himself. In other words, there is no absolute power inherent in the office of a king or ruler. The power that he may have is given by God through the approbation of the People.

For Rutherford there is a sacred responsibility between the governor and the governed. This relationship is reflective of God's covenant with mankind, but it is not identical. The covenant that God made with mankind is that what he required he provided through his only begotten son, our God and Savior Jesus Christ. In the covenant between King and people there is a sacred relationship, but it is grounded in the responsibility of the kingdom of God to rule for the benefit of the people. The King has an obligation to rule so that law and order may reign, peace may be secured, and justice roll down like water. The people, according to Scripture, have their obligation toward the king or any other governor. They — we — are to be godly subjects to the governing authorities. We should be praying for them and uplifting them.

Here is the beauty of a moral democracy. Democracy which is grounded in mutual submission is the best democracy. The relationship between husband and wife is a wonderful example of this. The husband lovingly gives himself for his wife. His wife responds in submissive love to her husband. Yet, both have obligations for the other. As each reaches toward the other such a dynamic brings about harmonious living.

Woe unto the public officials who take their offices without due care of the sacred responsibilities that they bear before Almighty God. Woe, also, to the people who do not pray for their governing authorities. It may be that God would judge them by sending them an ungodly ruler. Many times in history this has been a self-fulfilling judgment; as the people have wandered from the way of the Lord, they have elected for themselves governing authorities that do not consider the law of God. How fitting it is that King and people are both looking to God, looking to the other to fulfill their duty out of the blessings that God has given to them.

15

In what way is a king or other ruler said to be a "father" to the people of the land?

It is true that Aristotle taught that a kingly power is like unto a father's governing authority. However, Aristotle does not mean to say that they are the same. Indeed, Adam is a father to us all, yet he was not the king of the earth! Thus, we must deduce from both Scripture and natural law that a king may be like a father but is not the same as a father in a family.

In this question Rutherford deals with the matter of the King as a "father." An appeal has been made to Aristotle that kings are, in fact, fathers. There is no denial of a fatherly relationship by Rutherford. What is denied is that there is any analogical relationship similar to God and mankind. The relationship is not one of "generation," but of mutual submission. Thus, a ruler governs as a father, but he is as a father metaphorically, seeking the good of his children, the people who have consented that he might govern.

In a moral democracy nothing is more beautiful than the role of a magistrate who takes his job as that of a father. Yet, he does not assume an authoritative rule "like the Gentiles," but rather a governance that is derived from the charter made with Almighty God.

Many remember the great loss of the Challenger spacecraft. Many, also, remember the moving images of President Ronald Reagan embracing the families of those who had been lost in the tragic accident. I recall that many said that Reagan was "a father," or even, "a grandfather to the nation." For Rutherford, this would have been the perfect picture of a governing figure acting as a father. The same is true in the pastoral ministry. Pastors are fathers to their congregation, even as St. Paul said that he was. Yet, we are to call no man father. What gives? It is that we are to call no man father as if he is owed our submission by virtue of his creation order authority. Only God is our father. Our earthly fathers also demand such submission. But all others are fathers only in a metaphorical sense of lovingly providing what the children need.

16

Does monarchy or any other form of government headship justify despotic dominion over the people?

The king or other ruler does not have dominion and authority over the People by virtue of his office. He has only a fiduciary relationship, besides that covenantal relationship before God to serve them, protect them, and do good for them to the best of his ability and as God supports him to do so. Moreover, a ruler is not privileged to despotic dominion over a people's goods. The rights of ownership are from God. A free people must not surrender their rights to a government for those rights are not theirs to give or take. The divine rights of liberty are of God alone.

Rutherford takes up the matter of whether the king has a masterly relationship with his subjects. Rutherford denies this. His statement is powerful and is certainly biblical, and when applied to human government brings about extraordinary blessings. Rutherford says, "All men are born by nature of equal condition . . . The king has no proper, masterly, or lordly dominion over his subjects; his dominion is rather fiduciary and ministerial, than masterly."

A moral democracy is one in which the parties are bound together by a higher law. This law brings obligations to both the ruler and the ruled. But what is for certain is that the ruler does not rule by virtue of an inherent right. Therefore, governors and those who are governed live together by the divine right of mutual submission, not a divine right of subjugation. It is of great import that Rutherford stresses that liberty is a God-given right that cannot be surrendered. The People must be diligent in their citizenship to guard the divine rights of liberty, self-governance, private property ownership, and freedom of faith. The Rutherford vision of liberty recognizes the sinful possibility of a People surrendering the God-bestowed rights to a ruler in exchange for something else. This is as tyrannical as if a ruler were to grab those rights from the People. Both Ruler and People must recognize and guard the rights and responsibilities granted to them by God.

17

Does a head of government have autocratic, familial authority over his people or is his authority fiduciary only?

The power of the king is fiduciary, given to him directly by God in trust, but that trust is actually mediated to the king through the representation of the People. The People of a realm or nation do not "give themselves" to the king. The People allow a ruler to govern and, thus, owe him their lawful obedience by virtue of this free relationship. The king is, thus, not a father to the People, not a husband to the People, and even saying that he is a "tutor" is stretching it. The ruler is but a sort of "patron" to the People. The sacred bond between People and governor is made by free choice of the People and the ruler then acts with beneficence towards the governed. In a real sense, the Ruler is the servant of the People. He or she is a guard, to protect against evil. Governorship or earthly majesty is a sacred duty to God and the People.

The questions that Rutherford must address are in many ways nuanced. The matters are very closely associated. In question and answer 17 the matter is dealing again with the metaphorical and the analogical. Rutherford asserts that a king does not have an unbridled authority over the people. The king is not the husband per se. The king is not the father per se. The king is a tutor. And this tutor is given for the governance of the citizens. He is, as Rutherford says, "the watchman" of the people. The law that he uses to guard the people is a law that he is also subject to. We must remember that the husband has a great responsibility to love the wife as Christ loved the church. So even if the Royalists prefer to see the King in this husbandman role, it must be admitted that it is a role granted by a higher power and a role, not an ontological personhood, that is subject to God who made the role.

The best governments are those governments that are grounded upon the higher authority of God. The civil magistrate derives authority from God and exercises his duty as one under the law himself.

18

What is the nature of governmental leadership according to Scripture (1 Sam. 8: 9, 11)?

It is useless to try and distinguish between the ruling officer and the power delegated to that office. The power is either according to the law of God or not. However, the power of a king is never absolute by direction of Almighty God. To the contrary!

Rutherford quotes 1 Samuel 8:7-22. The passage is reproduced here for reference:

And the Lord said to Samuel, "Obey the voice of the people in all that they say to you, for they have not rejected you, but they have rejected me from being king over them. According to all the deeds that they have done, from the day I brought them up out of Egypt even to this day, forsaking me and serving other gods, so they are also doing to you. Now then, obey their voice: only you shall solemnly warn them and show them the ways of the king who shall reign over them."

So Samuel told all the words of the Lord to the people who were asking for a king from him. He said, "These will be the ways of the king who will reign over you: he will take your sons and appoint them to his chariots and to be his horsemen and to run before his chariots. And he will appoint for himself commanders of thousands and commanders of fifties, and some to plow his ground and to reap his harvest, and to make his implements of war and the equipment of his chariots. He will take your daughters to be perfumers and cooks and bakers. He will take the best of your fields and vineyards and olive orchards and give them to his servants. He will take the tenth of your grain and of your vineyards and give it to his officers and to his servants. He will take your male servants and female servants and the best of your young men and your donkeys, and put them to his work. He will take the tenth of your flocks, and you shall be his slaves. And in that day you will cry out because of your king, whom you have chosen for yourselves, but the Lord will not answer you in that day."

But the people refused to obey the voice of Samuel. And they said, "No! But there shall be a king over us, that we also may be like all the nations, and that our king may judge us and go out before us and fight our battles." And when Samuel had heard all the words of the people, he repeated them in the ears of the Lord. And the Lord said to Samuel, "Obey their voice and make them a king." Samuel then said to the men of Israel, "Go every man to his city."

With prodigious intellectual powers and an unsurpassed grasp of the original languages, the great Scottish divine demonstrates that the king is a king by the permission of Almighty God. The law that the king wields is a law derived from a higher power and is in no way intrinsic or inherent.

Moral democracies are composed of magistrates and citizens who recognize that the law is given to us just as the law was given to Moses and to the people of Israel. Moses was under the law as much as were the citizens of Israel. The law comes from God. The king is subject to the law every bit as much as the least person in the kingdom.

What is so remarkably clear in all these writings is this: to be a king or to be a citizen requires humility before Almighty God. And when such humility is assumed, we exercise our duties all the better.

19

Is the king or other governmental authority higher than the People in dignity and power? In what ways?

No, the king or other ruler is not above the people in any ontological sense. In a way, he is less than the People for he is their servant. On the other hand, there is an inherent dignity of civil offices that demands honor by the People who allow him to rule.

"The pilot is less than the whole passengers; the general less than the whole army; the tutor less than all the children; the physician less than all the living men whose health he cares for; the master or teacher less than all the scholars, because the part is less than the whole; the king is but a part and member (though I grant a very eminent and noble member) of the kingdom."

Here Samuel Rutherford lays out a blueprint for the relationship between governor and people. There is no intrinsic value or higher worth of one man over another. As Rutherford says, the general is not as important as the entire army. The general plays a particular part. He leads the Army to be sure. He conducts the campaigns necessary to bring about victory But he can only do so with willing and able troops. In a similar way, the least of these in the kingdom may be greater than the king himself. One cannot speak about a dignity in an ontological sense other than the dignity of the image of God in mankind. As Jacques-Benigne Bossuet (an extraordinarily gifted Roman Catholic homilist and defender of the divine right of kings) preached before King Louis XIV: "Kings reign supreme to me, says the eternal Wisdom, 'For me reges régnant' [Latin: "Kings rule"]; and from this we must conclude not only that the rights of royalty are established in its laws, but that the choice of the people is an effect of his Providence." There is no more effective debate tactic than the use of one's opponent against him. In this case, Bossuet says, "the choice of the people is an effect of his [God's] Providence" ("mais gue le choix des Personnes est un effet de sa Providence").

What a remarkably effective strategy by Rutherford and what a remarkable truth. This invaluable interpretation of the divine revelation of God made its way into the Constitution of the United States of America. It made its way into the constitutional rule of law in Great Britain and the other English-speaking nations and, indeed, the Commonwealth nations of the earth. It is made its way into other government forms whether constitutional monarchy or Republic.

This remarkable distillation of the Biblical teaching by Rutherford is a gift. The great Scottish divine points to the God-given dignity in all human beings. There is worth, value, intrinsic spark of the image of God that gives purpose and meaning in each of us. Therefore, we are quick to give honor to those who govern. However, we give honor to all human beings for we cannot speak of an inherent dignity apart from the image of God.

20

Are other governmental authorities appointed by the head of government "vicegerents" of God, as some think the king?

"Inferior judges," that is, civil servants, are no more vicars of God than the king or president. They are important, of course. However, they are but "deputies" of the ruler, on orders to carry out his programs of governance. There is honor and dignity in the deputy as there is with all those who serve the governed. However, they do not form a class or an aristocracy, a hierarchical order. They are servants of the People and servants of God.

The deputies of a king carry a derived power just as the king has a derived power from Almighty God mediated through the will of the people. Yet Rutherford once more draws a distinction between role, relationship, and ontological reality.

A moral democracy is necessarily composed of not only an executive branch of the government with its prime minister, president, or premier, but a bureaucracy of officials who carry out the will of the president or prime minister. Thus, they do have an authority that must be obeyed by the people intrinsically. However, once more, the bureaucracy owes their allegiance to the higher power that has ordained government.

The material covered in this exchange has a very timely import for our own day. We've seen excesses in what some have called "the deep state": those who are laboring in civil service assuming powers that are not their own and forgetting that their authority rests with the leader of the executive branch of government who was elected by the people. All of us must labor for better government for the glory of God.

21

What powers do the people's elected representatives have in relationship to the ruler of a nation?

The People's elected representatives, in a Republic or a Constitutional monarchy, are like unto the elders appointed by God to be judges. The People's representatives govern in a plurality that does not depend upon the king or other ruler. They are not mere advisors as some might say. Elected representatives have a legislative power while a king or other ruler has an executive power.

Samuel Rutherford advocates a federalism in which the lesser fiduciary and constitutional powers recognize their necessity for the good of mankind.

A federalism works best when there is proper deference between national, state, and local governments. The imposition of raw power supposed or assumed breaks the trust between these necessary levels of government. When this is so, the end of government is missed: to provide for free and productive people who are guarded by the levels of government in their inalienable rights.

Rutherford argues from Natural Law and Divine Revelation that governance through equally endowed branches of government follows a complimentary role relationship. Duly elected representatives in a parliament (or Congress) carry real authority, the Lord bless and keep you!; just as the king (or other "executive") plays his part.

The insights studiously gleaned and clearly proposed by Rutherford on the necessity of equal branches of government are nothing short of world-changing.

22

Are the powers of a head of state absolute or patterned after Natural Law and Special Revelation (the Holy Bible)?

The King is not absolute in his power, as witnessed by Scripture and by God's law written on our hearts and displayed in all of creation. The power to do ill to a king's subjects is surely not from God. Despotic authority is not of God, and is against justice, peace, reason, and natural law. Can a ruler use a supposed autocratic governing power granted by God, for example, to force a young lady to do his bidding? Of course not! For in truth, there is no demonstration or approbation of such autocratic power in either the Scriptures or in Natural Law. "An absolute power is contrary to nature, and so unlawful; for it makes the people give away the natural power of defending their life against illegal and cruel violence."

Nothing is clearer in the political theory and theological understanding of Samuel Rutherford than a divine prohibition against absolute authority. Thus, Rutherford:

A power contrary to justice, to peace and the good of the people, that looks to no law as a rule, and so is unreasonable, and forbidden by the law of God and the civil law, (L. 15. filius de condit. Instit.,) cannot be lawful power, and cannot constitute a lawful judge; but an absolute and unlimited power is such. How can the judge be the minister of God for good to the people (Rom. 13:4) if he have such a power as a king, given him of God, to destroy and waste the people?

Arg. 6. An absolute power is contrary to nature, and so unlawful; for it makes the people give away the natural power of defending their life against illegal and cruel violence, and makes a man who has need to be ruled and lawed by nature above all rule and law, and one who, by nature, can sin against his brethren such a one as cannot sin against any but God only, and makes him a lion and an unsocial man.

The power of this truth in seventeenth-century England, Scotland, Wales, and Ireland could not be harnessed. This young steed had to break free of the fence. It was an idea ready to explode upon the world. Indeed, the ideas of Rutherford about absolute power and the consent of the governed became a bedrock for the Constitution of the United States as well as constitutional monarchy in Great Britain and the Commonwealth of Nations. Moreover, it dealt a blow to absolute, autocratic power within the church. Roman Catholicism could no longer exist as it did before in England. Roman Catholicism would have to adapt to Rutherford's ideas in full bloom in North America (as did other monarchical ecclesiastical associations). Above and beyond Roman Catholicism, any concept of the absolute power of bishops in the Church of England was effectively degraded by Rutherford's *Lex, Rex.*

Absolute power resting in a single governor is, in fact, as Rutherford says, against the very witness of nature, much less forbidden in the divine revelation of the Holy Bible. Yet, tyrants continue to arrest power from those they govern, and autocrats continue their ruthless regimes. One of the reasons the Soviet Union was destined to fail was the concept of elitism. The dictator and those who served in his regime were taking under themselves the power that was not their own. It is no wonder then that the wall came down. But what was so powerfully learned in 1989 in 1990 has been forgotten by 2019. Therefore, the truth that Rutherford exposited and defended against the prelatic opponents remains a truth to be studied and a truth to be lifted up in our own day.

PART III

Lex, Rex
Questions 23-33

23

Is the king or other kind of ruler above the law that governs all others?

No, a king is not above the law of the land. To have prerogative above the law bestows an honor that is only due to One of infinite majesty. Absolute monarchy or any other form of unbridled government over the People is a guarantee for absolute evil. God's denouncement of absolutism in government is demonstrated in God's judgement on Nebuchadnezzar. He became God-like in his own self-assessment and was, therefore, reminded who is God and who is a mere man acting as a minister of God in human government (see Daniel 4:28-33, in which Nebuchadnezzar assumes to himself absolute monarchy; in 30-32 we read, "Is not this great Babylon, which I have built by my mighty power as a royal residence and for the glory of my majesty?" While the words were still in the king's mouth, there fell a voice from heaven, "O King Nebuchadnezzar, to you it is spoken: The kingdom has departed from you, and you shall be driven from among men, and your dwelling shall be with the beasts of the field. And you shall be made to eat grass like an ox, and seven periods of time shall pass over you, until you know that the Most High rules the kingdom of men and gives it to whom he will").

This question and response is the classic statement of how the law is king. The king is not the law. All are under the law. Rutherford appeals to the Biblical case of Babylonian King Nebuchadnezzar (reigned from 605-562 BC). The Babylonian king went mad after claiming sovereignty that led to remarkable gains in the Neo-Babylonian Empire (625-539

BC). Nebuchadnezzar had plenty to boast of. Babylon was the largest city in the world. Through a series of canal systems the land enjoyed a renewal and became a great agricultural center of the known world. Nebuchadnezzar's empire was the wealthiest political realm on earth. "Well might Nebuchadnezzar take pride in his construction of Babylon (Dan. 4.20), though such pride was his ultimate undoing."

Rutherford equates a modern ruler assuming absolute powers with the insanity of such an idea as seen in Nebuchadnezzar. There is no middle ground in the matter of absolute monarchy. Rutherford condemns such a government as unlawful before God and Natural Law.

What is so amazingly powerful about the 23rd question and answer is the advancement of the biblical concept of "the first shall be last and the last shall the first." The Apostle James instructed that those who would be ministers or teachers of the Gospel would receive a stricter judgement (James 3:1). Following on these deeply rooted biblical principles, Samuel Rutherford shows that the king actually has less freedom in his personal affairs than does the common man. In 24 points he delineates the great responsibilities that the king has which constrict and control his behavior much more so than one of his subjects.

In a moral democracy, public servants derive their power from the governed according to God's law placed into the heart of every human being. Indeed, it may be said that the principles that Rutherford exposits in this section rightly form the identity of the public servant in a moral democracy.

Ministers of the State as well as ministers of the Church do well to remember that the sacred responsibility of governing in God's institutions requires a sacrifice that is equal to the honor. Yet, how many today see public service as a route for political power, personal gain, or vanity? If the Word of God gives warning to ministers of Christ, shall we not also expect similar judgments for those who are his ministers in civil government? For the pastor cares for a flock of several hundred or several thousand. The minister of State might have millions or hundreds of millions of God-created souls in her care. The teaching of Rutherford on the restrictions of kingly office should be required for every official about to undertake any office of authority over others.

24

What, then, is the relationship of a head of state to the law of the land?

"For all the knights united cannot make one lord; and all the esquires united cannot make one knight; but all the people united made David king at Hebron. The king is above the people, by eminence of derived authority as a watchman, and in actual supremacy; and he is inferior to them in fountain-power, as the effect to the cause."

We have chosen to quote a portion of Rutherford's reply without modernization. The sentence is clear enough: the king is a king by the power of the People. Thus, he must be, like the People, under the same law of the land.

Samuel Rutherford's political theory concerning the king and the law is very much grounded in an Augustinian and in a Calvinistic understanding of mankind. It is not the king, according to Rutherford, who embodies the law. The law is a thing outside of the king. The law is a thing, more carefully put, that is over the king as well as over the subjects. The law is not inherent or intrinsic with the personhood of the king. Rutherford strongly advances this idea as he appeals to the sinfulness of mankind. How is it that the law can be equated with the very personhood of the king? It cannot. Rutherford says that all men are liars. Thus, the law is above the king as much as it is above any other man.

This was an essential article of political theory embedded in the founding of the American Republic. It remains a very central theme in every democracy that is grounded in the rule of law, in morality, even when the doctrine of the "depravity of Mankind" is not acknowledged.

25

How does a head of state relate to the "supreme law," that is, to protect the safety of the People?

"He is a minister by office, and one who receives honor and wages for this work, that, ex officio, he may feed his people. It is not an arbitrary power, but naturally tied and fettered to this same supreme law, salus populi, the safety of the people."

"Ex ungue leonem:" the lion is known by its claw. The kingly lion is identified by Rutherford, not as a vital power unto himself, but a power that is given by God for the protection of the people. This protection extends not only to personal safety and national security, but Rutherford, in his British context, reminds the earthly sovereign that he or she must be a guardian of the People in matters related to religion and to morals. This is not a theonomic initiative by Rutherford, but rather, the truth of the law over the king by way of its call for the ruler to be a repository of guardianship. He holds this power not for himself, first, but for the People.

What is most beautiful in the political theory that undergirds any democratic and free nation is its enormous presumption of self-sacrifice on the part of the rulers (as well as the prayerful submission by the subjects). Nothing is seemlier than a public servant who sees his role as a vocation, lived out as unto God. Nothing decorates the presence of a citizen more in such a moral democracy than to utter the names of the officers of government in public and private prayer.

26

Can the king or other ruler of a human government ever truly be above the law of the land?

God does not make a ruler in order to possess a "royal stamp" to give him the power to do as he pleases. He is a ruler of the People because God has allowed it through the mediation of the will of the governed.

"Because the king by nature is not king, as is proved; therefore, he must be king by a politic constitution and law; and so the law, in that consideration, is above the king, because it is from a civil law that there is a king rather than any other kind of governor."

Here we have the veritable "tenderloin" of Rutherford's political philosophy. In answering the assertions that the king is the law by his own supposed sovereignly appointed rule (and, thus, his very person) the eminent Scottish theologian demonstrates from divine relation, natural law, and common practice, that the king cannot possibly order the consciences of People, much less their response to the Higher Law of God.

Moral democracy holds that there is a greater Law and that is the Law of God, the "natural law" that is within every creature. We, thus, acknowledge the Author of the Law, and show our dependence upon Him in all things. The first subject of this Law is the governor, the king, or the president. When the King recognizes the Kingship of Almighty God and bows in reverence before the Lord in his own life it is a happy harbinger of abundant blessings to come. Let us therefore pray for our civil leaders to receive Jesus Christ, to follow Him, and to quickly acknowledge His supremacy in all things.

27

Is it true that the king or other rule is the sole, supreme, and final interpreter of the Law?

"The king is not the sole and final interpreter of the law." Neither king, president, prime minister, or their civil servants are the final interpreters of the law. Psalm 2:10 states, "Be wise now therefore, O ye kings, be instructed, ye judges of the earth." God rebukes those besides the king or executive who do judge from the law unfairly (Ps. 82:1-5; 58:1-2; Isa. 1:17, 23, 25, 26; 3:14; Job 29:12-15; 31:21-22.). The last voter in a senate is not the sole judge, else why should there be other senators? The law of the land is not interpreted by any one man, but by a plurality of wise judges set apart through the ordinary mechanisms of representative government.

Thus, we observe Rutherford's teaching for the robed branch of government: the Court.

The concept of checks and balances that is embedded in Western democracies is an essential and wise presumption in government; "Trust but verify" is an unquestionably straightforward Biblical principle. That divinely revealed principle, in Calvinistic theology named, "depravity," states that the image of God in humankind is marred by the Fall (Adam and Eve's disobedience to God in the Garden of Eden). Our first parents' disobedience brought not only immediate and personal consequences to Adam and Eve, but also cosmic and "federal" (or representative) consequences to all people (and Creation). Thus, depravity of the human soul, which must be redeemed by Christ. Even then, however, depravity remains as a virus capable of breaking out again. So, a solemn, healthy suspicion is both warranted and wise (for the residual effects of depravity remain, though they are atoned for and are being "treated" by the means of grace throughout a believer's life). Moral government must be built on this irreplaceable foundation. A moral democracy is a democracy in which there are laws, natural laws or a recognition of the truthfulness of the biblical law, that acknowledge man is fallen. Moreover, man neither by his status (such as a king) or by his sanctification ever reaches a point in which he may be the sole arbiter of laws. Thus, our Supreme Court is made of a plurality, not a single justice. Moreover, dissenting justices have the right to voice their dissent.

The time in which we live is a very dangerous era. Increasingly, singular voices are taking under themselves the rights and privileges of the plurality. We have seen in recent decades the strengthening of the executive branch of government to the detriment of the other branches. The framers of the Constitution held that legislation in only one branch to the neglect of the others represents an active tyranny. Likewise, in our churches, the seriousness about ecclesiastical polity has led to extraordinary cases of abuse. The Protestant churches no longer need to look to Rome and to monarchial prelate. They have only to look to the Empire-building television personalities and Crusade miracle workers — so-called — to see the rotten fruit of absolute monarchy. It is high time that many of us in the church repent and return to a biblical form of government in which there is no single power judging over the other voices. Today every institution of human endeavor would benefit from this fundamental principle of plural government and suspicion of self-isolating, rigid, and dangerous individualism. Leadership without accountability always leads to ruin in the life and family of the lone wolf leader, as well as the constituents he or she should be serving.

28

Is it lawful and allowable by divine and natural law for subjects or citizens of a government to defend themselves against despotic rule, by force if necessary?

"We obey the king for the law, and not the law for the king."

Rutherford is at his absolute best in defending the rights of the people against a tyrannical king and in asserting their right, if and when necessary, to take up arms in defense of their families and their properties. Or, shall we say, rather, that a tyrannical man who carries a title therefore has unbridled privilege to abuse his subjects? The answer in both Scripture and in nature is a resounding, "Nay!"

A moral democracy is one in which elected rulers, or if by cause of a constitutional monarchy those who have received their title by birth, are subject to the people in every way. There is a contractual agreement between the governors and those who are governed. This agreement has within it the laws of nature and the laws revealed in God's own word: that we do not lord over subjects like the Gentiles of old. But the rulers are given the God-appointed work of defending their subjects and executing justice against evil that would seek to hurt their subjects. But when rulership becomes despotic it is not only the right of the man to speak out against such a monstrous aberration, but to defend his family and his rights.

29

In cases of hostility of a king against his own people, is there a distinction between an officeholder and a man?

An office is given honor. But a man that holds that office may, indeed, be a vile individual who is unworthy of the office. Thus, the office does not make the man. Though God has called us to obey lawful authorities, we are not to obey those who command sin. We obey the king for the law. We do not obey the law for the king. Pilate's power to crucify Christ was not a lawful power given to the Roman governor by God.

This is a very important vein running in the goldmine of Rutherford's political thought. It is what makes Samuel Rutherford the most balanced in his appreciation of citizen rights and restraints. Nero, Rutherford argues, should not be overthrown merely for his paganism (he may be impeached by the will of the people). But he must be resisted without fail should he command a Christian to worship the idol. The muddleheaded thinking of some so-called believers who have taken the law into their own hands to execute judgment against officials who tolerate sin is abhorrent to the Word of God into the foundations of a moral democracy. Such perpetrators of evil must be punished to the fullest extent of the law. Anarchy waits in the wings if it is not so. Conversely, we have seen in our own society that we are getting perilously close to a possible time when an immoral government in Western democracies could order a Christian to violate the word and the law of God. The believer, by the studious considerations of Samuel Rutherford as well as the founders themselves, would have no other choice but to disobey and to say with Saint Peter, "shall I obey God or man?"

The foundations of moral democracy rest upon the rights of the governed. The laws of our nation may be bent to tolerate sin but never can they be imposed upon the innocent. It matters not whether that citizen is a Muslim, a Christian, or Hindu. The government of a truly moral democracy, one built upon the principles of *Lex, Rex*, would not and could not impose violations of the conscience of the individual.

30

Are those citizens of a tyrannical government called to a passive obedience? And what if they flee the despotic powers? Is that lawful by God and Nature (the revelation written on our hearts and observed as "common sense")?

While the Apostle Peter, in 1 Peter 2:18, admonishes the people to show patience and bear up under persecution, and while Jesus' own non-resistance is a virtue for us, yet these do not require that we give up self-defense. We must resist if given an unlawful order. If one flees in order to obey God rather than Man, this is not a sin.

This section deals with yet another clarification between suffering quietly beneath injustice and fleeing from injustice and brutality, as well as opposing. The followers of Christ are the best subjects even in the most horrible conditions. Yet the standard of Christ's necessary passive obedience does not require the believer to seek to exercise that which Christ did in that passive obedience. Christ was becoming a sacrifice for sin. That is not the calling of the believer. Those who stand in opposition to governments which persist in brutality or, alternatively, flee from the stronger tyrannical power, can in no way be chastised on the basis of Christ's passivity.

31

Can self-defense against tyranny be justified in the Bible?

Self-preservation in all creatures is the norm. The bull defends itself by the horns. The eagle defends herself with her claws and her bill. A lamb cannot defend itself against a wolf, so the lamb runs away. That running away is, in fact, an act of self-defense. Some say that David refused to kill Saul because Saul was the Lord's anointed. Yet, Saul was allowed by the People through their representatives. David's restraint, when he had opportunity to kill his enemy, was an act of godly and strategic wisdom. David was on the run from Saul. He was defending his life. That he did not turn the defense into an offensive operation does not prove that an oppressed people must continue to be oppressed without any redress.

The tyrannical invasion of 1640 to force a people to adhere to a different form of worship, after the bad counsel of Archbishop William Laud, surely one of the most atrocious ecclesiastical leaders of the English church, justified resistance and, where necessary, fleeing to America or to the continent. So Rutherford once again brilliantly dissects the word of the Lord. David's patience and his long-suffering under despotic rule could not be equated with an absolutist government that sought to impose its will on the consciences of its subjects. Those are two altogether different things.

We would do well to follow Rutherford and his careful study of the Word of God. We would benefit in our churches and in our civil governments if we were to thoughtfully consider the nuances, the comparisons and the contrasts between biblical examples and present realities.

32

Does the Word of God allow for the People to resist a tyrannical power?

David defended himself against king Saul and it is clear in 1 Chronicles 12:22-34 that an entire army joined with David to resist Saul's attempts to kill David. Indeed, the Spirit of the Lord commends David for his resistance to this evil as we read throughout the entire Biblical account.

Rutherford must exercise his careful study of the Word of God to refute the assertion that biblical examples deny the rights of the oppressed to defend themselves. Rutherford demonstrates that it is God who delegates authority to human rulers. We are to give honor unto these laws and unto these lawgivers and law enforcers because we are, in truth, giving honor and obedience unto the Lord. However, whenever any earthly ruler not merely disobeys God but directly orders people to do that which is forbidden by divine law or natural law, the people have no other recourse but to resist or to flee.

One of the great challenges within Western Christianity today is its knowledge of the Bible. Since the Bible is no longer taught in government schools, and since, it may be said even with charity, that the amount of holy Scripture that is read or preached in many evangelical churches is meager, we all stand in danger of misinterpreting Scripture and receiving the terrible just reward for our ignorance. Jesus Christ said that the truth shall set you free. Conversely, ignorance of the truth of the Word of God places one in bondage. When such ignorance is codified it leads to unavoidable and inevitable oppression. There can be no greater throwing off of the chains of oppressive government than to revive the diligent study of the Word of God in our homes, in our churches, and in our places of educating the young.

33

Does Romans 13:1 negate the lawfulness of self-defense against tyrannical government?

"Let every person be subject to the governing authorities. For there is no authority except from God, and those that exist have been instituted by God."

No. Romans 13 is speaking of lawful authorities and powers. Whenever the Roman government officials ordered Peter and the disciples to disobey God, by not preaching, the men obeyed God rather than Man. Indeed, the power of any government (from a parent to an employer to a king or president) is drawn from the honor of the Lord. Whenever such powers order the People to do what is forbidden, they become tyrants and must be disobeyed. This is not in any way violating Romans 13.

One of the remarkable features of the scholarly work of Rutherford is his careful exegesis and application of Scripture. In this case, those supporting a divine right of kings had appealed to the famous holy text on the subject of believers and civil authorities, Romans chapter thirteen. Since, in that passage, St. Paul asserts that civil authorities are his "ministers" for good and to be entrusted with the power of the sword to punish evil, proponents of autocratic government feel justified in defending their cause. Rutherford carefully distinguishes between the meaning of the text in relationship to other texts. He not only avoids the error of the heretics and the ill-trained, but, indeed, shows cognitive adroitness in differentiating, dissecting, and discriminating when handling the sacred Word. Could Paul have meant that all authorities, regardless of their abuse of office, must be obeyed, even if they command the believer to do what is against the will of God? The answer is clearly "no." By comparing Scripture to Scripture, clarifying ostensibly obscure passages with the indubitably clear, Rutherford makes the greater application to the relationship of the Church with civil government. The situation is clear for Christians today: we must pray for and honor those who serve in civil government for the sake of obedience to God. However, when civil government requires a believer to do that which is against God's revealed will, the believer has no choice but to either resist, flee, or disobey. This action is to be distinguished from civil authority that may be antagonistic towards Christianity or legislating code that stands against the revealed Word of God. It is not until the government requires the believer to bow to the unlawful order that resistance and disobedience must follow. A great example of this is seen in Roe versus Wade in the United States. The infamous 1973 Supreme Court decision rendered an unbiblical position. If, God forbid, an autocratic government official required you to have your wife or daughter abort an unborn child, then you would have no choice but to resist, flee, or disobey. That is far different from living in a country which allows it. Such careful scholarship not only marked the mind and pen of Samuel Rutherford, but it must also increasingly reflect the average churchman today. We have many distractions. However, the stakes are far too high for us to be distracted from this essential task of studying and rightly dividing the word of truth. It will be the foolish and disobedient who failed to distinguish and recognize the teaching of Scripture who will be led away in chains of their own making.

PART IV

Lex, Rex
Questions 34-44

34

Can those who believe in the divine right of monarchy believe that when such a king becomes tyrannical that the people cannot defend themselves?

"We obey parents, masters, kings, upon this formal ground, because they are God's deputies, and set over us not by man, but by God; so that not only are we to obey them because what they command is good and just, (such a sort of obedience an equal owes to the counsel of either equal or inferior,) but also by virtue of the fifth commandment, because of their place of dignity." If parents become murderers, must the child remain obedient? No, it is clear in both Scripture and in the Laws written on our hearts that we must not obey tyrannical powers.

Samuel Rutherford demonstrates his considerable pastoral and scholarly skills in a simple answer to this matter of a People and their representatives defending themselves against the king: "The wife is obliged to bed and board with her husband, but not if she fear he will kill her in the bed."

I have seen in pastoral ministry where some battered women have come to me saying that their minister had told them that they must remain because of Ephesians 5 and other passages related to the role relationships of husbands and wives. But Christ Himself, says Rutherford, avoided Herod until it was the right time for the sacrifice. And Peter in Acts 4 shows us that we must obey God and not Man whenever the two laws collide.

35

Are the sufferings of the martyrs in the early church proof against defensive actions in the case of governmental tyranny?

Those who point to the martyrs in the early church as proof that Christians should be not be able to defend themselves against tyrannical authorities "proveth nothing." However, we admit that there are church fathers, like Cyprian, who say, "Christians cannot, by violence, defend themselves against persecutors." Can this really be so? If a murderer were to come against Cyprian seeking the father's life, should Cyprian, then, defend himself? The answer is self-evident. Others, like Tertullian, make statements that both sides can quote. We prefer the saying of Theodoret (393-458) (fol. 98, De providentia, or Ten Discourses on Providence) that "evil men reign through the cowardliness of the subjects." I might also cite Christians in France, Holland, and Germany in Luther's day; and also Calvin, Beza, and others who deny that martyrdom is necessary rather than defense.

Again we are witness to the extraordinary mind of Rutherford. How many of us would take on the church fathers, like Tertullian or Cyprian, and say that they are wrong about the application of Scripture? But Rutherford did. Yet, he cited other trusted figures in church history to demonstrate that martyrdom is not to be necessarily preferred over resistance to autocratic authorities. Time and place, situation and tyrant, all present themselves with numerous variables to consider. As with so much of Scripture, wisdom is necessary to apply the truth. Once more the reminder from Rutherford, at this point, is to be exact in our interpretation of the Word of God before admonishing others.

36

Is the authority to wage war only vested in the supreme ruler of a nation?

The power of the sword is granted to the king by the People. The Parliament mediates the responsibilities associated with bearing arms. A monarch is not isolated in his decision-making concerning war. The king is not even a co-equal with parliament on the matter of waging war. He is subordinate. He may give his recommendation, but the legislators must rightfully vote in plurality for such a grave matter.

I read Rutherford and wonder if I am reading the Constitution of the United States. For the War Powers Acts in Article I, Section 8, Clause 11 of the US Constitution grants Congress the power to declare war. The President, meanwhile, derives the power to direct the military after a Congressional declaration of war from Article II, Section 2, which names the President Commander-in-Chief of the armed forces. While several notable cases come to mind in which the Commander-in-Chief deployed combat personnel in military operations (and the War Powers Resolution of 1973 sought to clarify this anomaly that has become almost commonplace), the fact remains that the Constitution does not give unlimited power to the Executive Branch. In this, as in so many other matters, Samuel Rutherford searched Scripture and observed Natural Law through the lens of Aristotle and others to arrive at his conclusion.

The matter is of importance in many areas of life and governance. The pastor of a church, for example, must not be given a free reign in deploying the funds of the parish church for new buildings or other major programs outside of the approved budget. The minister is not merely co-equal, at this point, with the Session or other lowest adjudicatory body, but is subordinate to them. Why? Rutherford's teaching is that an executive branch of a governing body cannot act outside of the authority granted to him by the People's duly elected representatives. Many pastors have brought pain on themselves and their congregations by ignoring or defying this truth of God rightly discerned by Rutherford.

37

Is it Biblically lawful for the powers of Scotland to defend their brethren, the protestants of England, against cavaliers?

[Is it just for nations to rise in arms to defend other nations under siege of evil?]

Neighbors must help neighbors. This is a natural law and Biblical law known by all. Some say that this is prohibited when doing so against the king who has the God-given power of the sword. Yet, a "host of men helped David against king Saul (1 Chronicles 12:18)" and, therefore, "entered in a lawful war." When a King unlawfully wields the weapon of war against the Parliament and the People, such a monarch ceases to enjoy the blessing of God and has become a power unto himself. Tyranny forfeits the God-ordained covering of a ruler. Tyranny breaks the sacred covenant and obligations of that covenant between Prince and People. One part of Britain must help another part of Britain if that brother is under siege of a foreign power. If an Islamic band invaded a part of Britain, surely the other parts would rise to their defense and be recognized as legitimate in doing so. The current situation in which a king has assumed absolute power (and, thus, has forfeited his lawful magisterial rights before God and Man) is no different from a foreign power invading Britain.

So, "Yes," neighbor must help neighbor against the autocratic and despotic authorities who ignore or knowingly disobey both nature and Scripture concerning their limited powers.

The teaching of Rutherford in answer to the Cavaliers (the party that supported absolute monarchy and, thus, supported the increasing tendencies of James I of Scotland and, then, Charles I of the consolidated realm) is textbook political philosophy for foreign relations in our day. The Rutherford principle is to carefully weigh whether the "neighbor" in trouble with the authorities is actually suffering from despotism or merely in disagreement with policy. This is not a distinction without a difference, but rather is the crux of the matter. We can easily rush to the support of a neighbor, a nation, or a group whose citizens or members are claiming victimization at the hands of tyranny. "The law of nature," says Rutherford, teaches us to be obedient in "acts of charity." However, it is no help to God's cause to assist in revolt against a power that may be immoral, corrupt, or malodorous, yet is not ordering the People to disobey the Lord and His laws written on our hearts. Conversely, Rutherford demonstrates that it is altogether reasonable and righteous to aid a neighbor or nation in defense against an abusive power that uses its reign as a terror against humanity.

Of equal interest and importance is that Rutherford demonstrates that a civil authority that has assumed totalitarian powers is no less than a foreign invader.

38

Is monarchy the best form of human government?

There is a sense in which all governments are monarchical in one way or the other. "An absolute and unlimited monarchy is not only the best form of government, but it is the worst." Jesus Christ is King without parliament. But human kings do need checks and balances. The sinful propensity of our nature dictates it. "What is one man under no restraint, but made a god on earth, and so drunk with the grandeur of a sinning-god, here under the moon and clouds?" However, monarchy, with its necessary limits and restraints, "is the best government absolutely, because God's immediate government must be best." Yet we must remember that Parliaments and Kings do err. There is no perfect government here on earth.

Constitutional monarchy is clearly the preferred political system of Rutherford. Some have said that a People may be more disposed to one form or another because of history, culture, or experience. If this is so, then the failure of Cromwell's Commonwealth of England may be partially explained by the "natural" urge of the Englishman (Scot, Welshman, and Irishman) to a constitutional monarchy. While Rutherford advocates constitutional monarchy in his own land, he wisely does not calculate his conclusions so that all other nations must be as Britain. The principles of good governance remain unchanged whether there is a republic or a constitutional monarchy. Rutherford would agree with Aristotle that a pure democracy is as troublesome as a pure and absolute monarchy. Governance by mob rule, by the loudest or the strongest, will devolve into anarchy. Alternatively, all forms of government may rightly appropriate the truth of God into their political systems and enjoy some measure of divine blessing.

39

Does the king or head of state retain powers above the law of the land?

Jure regalia is that right of a king that transcends private ownership. Such rights are not directly from God. If such rights exist for a monarch, they do exist because the People have allowed it. The king does not retain powers above the law of the land. He, like all, is subject to the law. The law is king.

In Britain that which does not belong to individuals or their corporate structures do belong, by law, to the Crown. However, only the most unreasonable Monarchist would say that the right to, for example, a river or a field, is jure regalia by nature. The Crown may indeed have ownership of a given property, as the German government or the US Government may claim ownership of, for example, a national forest. But this ownership is by law. We have witnessed, however, despicable instances of "nationalizing" property without the consent of the governed. This is an act of dictatorial power and must be condemned. Private ownership, according to Rutherford, is to be deduced from both Natural Law and Special Revelation (the Bible).

"To [Aristotle] the Individual is the primary reality, and has the first claim to recognition. In his metaphysics, individual things are regarded not as the mere shadows of the idea, but as independent realities; universal conceptions not as independent substances but as the expression for the common peculiarity of a number of individuals. Similarly in his moral philosophy he transfers the ultimate end of human action and social institutions from the State to the individual, and looks for its attainment in his free self-development. The highest aim of the State consists in the happiness of its citizens."

40

In what ways do the People have rights above the rights of the king or supreme ruler of a nation?

*Aristotle wrote, "A tyrant seeks his own, a king the good of the subjects; for he is no king who is not content and excelling in goodness" (Aristotle, **Ethics**).*

To answer the question, let us consider a father and a son. Natural Law and Scripture both confirm the subordinate role relationship of the son to the father. But let us say that the father and son enter into a sales agreement. In this agreement, the son sells a piece of land to the father for an agreed amount. Now, even though the father is clearly a natural superior to his son, according to the laws of the land, that father has become a subordinate to his son in terms of law. He owes the son money. What if the father takes advantage of his privileged role relationship? Let us suppose that he refuses the pay the debt. He keeps the land and refuses further dealing. The son protests. The son goes to the sheriff. He shows the law enforcement officer the bill of sale. The sheriff sends a deputy to speak to the father and to seek to mediate the dispute. But as he arrives at the door, the father tells the deputy, "Now, look here! I am his dad, for goodness sake. He is my son. I was here before that boy was a glimmer in the eye of his mother. He may be thirty years of age, but I am still his old man. Therefore, I need not pay this bill." What do you think the sheriff's deputy will do? Will he say, "You know, that is a good argument. This bill of sale is worthless!"? Of course not! He will respond that the father owes the son. "I don't care about any glimmer in your eye or his mother's! All I know is what I see on this bill of sale. Sir, you need to pay up! You are in your son's debt! He has got it over on you on this one. Pay up!"

Yes, I have taken vast liberties in my summary of Rutherford. But this is a central argument in question forty. And of all the things that Rutherford wrote about that relationship, nothing rings truer than the father-son relationship.

In a similar way, we may say that the president of the United States has a higher position than I do. And that would be absolutely correct. He has my respect. I also owe him my taxes! However, the president of the United States cannot use his relationship of honor to defraud me. That would be against the law. Once more, Rutherford is pointing us to the supremacy of the law over any supposed position of honor. Question 40 and its answer is an incredible admission of common sense. However, the history of, for instance, the twentieth century is stained with the blood of those who suffered under the dictatorial powers of those who deny this common sense. Sin is a despicable parasite that feeds on the host of love and relationship.

41

Are Roman Catholic doctrines of church governance being used to formulate policy as to the self-defense of a People against tyranny?

[Is it right to use monarchial church law to dictate what is right or wrong in terms of national self-interest?]

"Dominion is founded upon grace." It is not right to use such a law upon the colonists in America. Shouldn't the colonists have the right to choose their own government? If they are bound to the King let it be by grace, not prelatic power and force.

Rutherford uses the colonists in America in two instances: in this question and the next (forty-two). The post Counter-Reformation Roman Catholic church looks quite different in many ways to the Roman Church of Rutherford's Day. Yet the arguments made remain valid when we see that Rutherford's assertions are made in context. We make good use of this question by focusing on the universal truth that Rutherford displays: namely, that a relationship between Prince and People, between any civil government and its citizens, must be grounded in a mutual agreement of respect and honor. A marriage, a friendship, a business relationship, or any other covenantal agreement, is best undertaken when the currency is mutual honor and respect.

42

Are Christian kings and rulers immediately under the governance of Jesus Christ and not the People?

The civil authorities cannot be over the Church of Jesus Christ. They cannot be considered vice-regents with Christ, for they are men and are elected or given allowance by the People to govern in terms of this physical world. They are under Christ in terms of being responsible to Him for their use of the privilege of governance. But it is impossible for a king to be called the head of the Church, for only Jesus Christ is the head of the Church.

Maxwell, who wrote the polemic advocating the divine right of kings, provoked Rutherford with this matter. Since a ruler is a Christian, and since kings and others in authority, are "God's ministers" (Romans 13:4-6), doesn't it follow that this Christian ruler is answerable directly to Jesus? The proposition begs the question (in the logical and syllogistic sense of that phrase). In other words, any logical follow-up to the proposition will be wrong for the central idea is fallacious. The answer, according to Rutherford, is clearly, "No! The Christian king is allowed to govern by the People. He cannot be a pretender to the crown rights of King Jesus!" Yes, we must add: the believing ruler is a unique and wonderful entity in the governance of the land (unless he is unwise, in which case it is better to have a heathen wiseman to govern). But his faith and his office do not combine to give a super-power supplanting the role of the parish and the pastor, and any adjudicatory within the earthly Church of our Lord.

One caveat should be made. While a monarch may have responsibility for the faith (or as a president and Congress has responsibility to enforce the First Amendment, giving Christians and other faiths the right to express their faith), as the Monarch of the United Kingdom is the head of the Church of England, such a ceremonial arrangement is far from the tyrannical situation that Rutherford and other believers faced in the seventeenth-century.

43

How about the King of Scotland?
Is he above the law of the land?

[Are there exceptional cases where a king or other head of state is above the law?]

No. The King of Scotland [James VI of Scotland (1566-1625)] is not above the governmental structures of Scotland or above any of the laws. The King is beneath the Parliament and the Law. The King is certainly not the head of the Church of Scotland. He governs only by the will of the People of Scotland through the mediation of the Parliament.

James VI was a remarkably able king. Some thought he was the most effective monarch since William the Conqueror. His relationship to Scotland did not give him any special dispensation with Rutherford. Whether James VI or Scotland or James I of England (over all Great Britain, as James would put it), he was, still, a man who served as monarch and, therefore, by Scripture and Natural Law, a man under the law as any other person.

44

Summary remarks on the divine right of kings, shown to be against the Bible and against the law of nature, and the Scriptural and natural law revelation: the Law is supreme, not the king. Authority in human government is derived, according to Scripture and Nature, from the universal rights of the governed.

1. *Monarchy can be a good form of government, and, perhaps, the very best in its limited expression. However, that does not mean that other polities are in error. They rise or fall by their adherence to God's laws.*

2. *Royalty is from lineage only if the People allow such a system. There is no intrinsic virtue or nobility. Any such nobility is merely granted by Law.*

3. *God has ordained human government for the good of humankind. However, a king is not more "natural" than any other ruler.*

4. *It is denied that there should be one supreme ruler in a nation.*

5. *Absolute monarchy is not, as some think, a "ray and beam of divine majesty" come down from heaven.*

6. *Parliament, like a King, can abuse power. Both are responsible to the People. All are under the Law.*

7. *A coronation is a ceremony. It is not a heavenly event. It is to be entered into with prayer and with honor by the People. But a coronation does not bestow any power beyond what the People have expressed in the Law allowing the coronation.*

In *Lex, Rex*, Rutherford uses question and answer forty-four to not merely summarize, but to address diverse subsidiary questions related to the main point. I have listed seven matters. Rutherford listed twenty. However, many of them continue to address contemporary concerns. The universal teaching is established: a ruler is under the law. Though we owe honor unto the civil government, we do not owe obedience to an unlawful order. The civil authorities, likewise, do serve, not reign. The governors have a responsibility to protect the People and promote their general welfare. Their privilege of rule is tempered with a heavier responsibility to both God and the People. The warning given to prospective ministers of the Gospel is to be charged to those seeking public office in government:

"Not many of you should become teachers, my brothers, for you know that we who teach will be judged with greater strictness" (James 3:1).

With great privilege comes great responsibility. The high calling of leadership for the people, whether in the Church or in the State or in any other enterprise, private or public, requires that the leader be the servant of all. This remains the first and the supreme test of true leadership:

"The greatest among you shall be your servant" (Matthew 23:11).

Afterword

As we have gone through the 44 questions and answers, the careful reader has no doubt noticed several exigent features:

- The somewhat foreign and inaccessible situations that prompted Rutherford's replies, a point that I will address momentarily
- The prodigious depth and breadth of Rutherford's biblical theology and his adroit use of both Scripture and logic, history and political thought, and theological reflection and critical thinking, to both answer his critics and advance the articles of liberty
- The single-mindedness of Samuel Rutherford's treatise: not only is the king duty-bound and responsible to the same law as his subjects, his right to reign is not a divine right but a contractual relationship; he governs by virtue of the consent of the governed. Indeed, I found myself thinking at each question, as I prepared for a brief commentary on the section, that in a way we were saying the same thing each chapter. But rather than being a critique of a supposed redundancy, the present writer finds this a remarkable ability of Rutherford to stay "on point."

As I reflect on my time with Rutherford and my concern for the reader, I am very aware of the great distance between ourselves and seventeenth-century England, Wales, Scotland, and Ireland. The realm was embroiled in an unprecedented English Civil War—coined at once a "Great Rebellion," "Puritan Revolution," "English Revolution," and "War of Religion" depending upon your historical and political perspective—that threatened the stability of a veritable hegemonic power. The Cavaliers, representing Charles I and the royalist party (the party that provoked Rutherford's political thinking), were in a way more unified than the Roundheads, who represented the Parliament.

The challenge of the Parliamentary forces and the Puritan party was the extraordinary degree of social, political, and religious divisiveness within its ranks - from the villainous severity of Major General Thomas Harrison (who signed the warrant for the execution of Charles I) in the Fifth Monarchist Movement, to the libertarian movements like the Ranters, to the more moderate voices of democracy like the Levelers, to the experimental communist groups like the Diggers. All of this can be overwhelming for us today. On top of that the sides would change. The Scottish Covenanters, so important to the Westminster Assembly, would later regard the English Puritan movement has having gone too far with the regicide of Charles I. The Restoration of Charles II to the throne, thus ending the short-lived Commonwealth of England, could not have happened without Scottish Covenanter aid.

All these things led to this book. Thus, we pray, that in some way, the theological, Biblical, and political thought of one of the great minds (and hearts) of Western Civilization (and one so important to the rise of Constitutional Monarchy in Great Britain and to the founding of the United States of America and to the expression of liberty in the Commonwealth of Nations) could be, at least in some small way, accessible. For we need a revival of trust in the One to whom Rutherford looked in order to claim and reclaim the social, political, and force-of-life realities that He promised would flow from such faith:

"And ye shall know the truth, and the truth shall make you free" (John 8:32, King James Version of the Holy Bible).

M.A.M.

Bibliography

Adamo, Thomas. "Lex Rex. The Law, The King." *Lakehurst, NJ: Woodbine Cottage* (2010).

Adkins, Arthur WH. "II. The Connection between Aristotle's Ethics and Politics." *Political Theory* 12, no. 1 (1984): 29–49.

Adshead, J. The Progress of Religious Sentiment, the Advancement of the Principles of Civil and Religious Freedom, Etc. s.n., 1852. https://books.google.com/books?id=Yzc3AAAAMAAJ.

Aitken, P. Henderson. Edited by Robert Gilmour. *The Scottish Historical Review* 2, no. 7 (1905): 324–324. http://www.jstor.org/stable/25517634.

Alexander, W. An Abridgment of the Acts of the Parliaments of Scotland: From the Reign of James the First in 1424 to the Union with England in 1707, Including Verbatim All the Acts Now in Force and Use ; with Notes and References, and an Appendix Containing a Chronological Table of the Titles of the Whole Acts and Statutes Passed by the Scottish Parliaments. Black, 1841. https://books.google.com/books?id=0HgDAAAAQAAJ.

Althusius, Johannes. "Politica Methodice Digesta of Johannes Althusius (Althaus)" (1932).

Anstey, Peter R. John Locke Vol. IV, Vol. IV,. London: Routledge, 2006.

Aquinas, Thomas. "Commentary on Aristotle's De Anima, Trans." Foster, Kenelm & Humphries, Silvester, Notre Dame: Dumb Ox Books (1994).

Armitage, David. The Declaration of Independence: A Global History. Harvard University Press, 2007.

———. "The Declaration of Independence and International Law." *The William and Mary Quarterly* 59, no. 1 (2002): 39–64.

Arraj, Jim, and David George Mullan. *Scottish Puritanism*, 1590-1638. Oxford University Press on Demand, 2000.

Aylmer, Gerald Edward. *The Levellers in the English Revolution*. Ithaca, NY: Cornell University Press, 1975.

Bacon, Francis. *New Atlantis*. At the University Press, 1900.

———. "Novum Organum, Trans." *Chicago: Open Court* (1994).

Bacon, Francis, and Basil Montagu. The Works of Francis Bacon, Lord Chancellor of England. Vol. 1. Parry & McMillan, 1854.

Bamberg, Stanley. "A Footnote to the Political Theory of John Adams." *Vindiciae Contra Tyrannos* (1996).

Barker, A. E. *Milton and the Puritan Dilemma*, 1641-1660. University of Toronto Press, Scholarly Publishing Division, 1976. https://books.google.com/books?id=WzREDAAAQBAJ.

Barnes, Thomas Garden. The Laws and Liberties of Massachusetts: Reprinted from the Copy of the 1648 Edition in the Henry E. Huntington Library. Legal Classics Library, Division of Gryphon Editions, 1982.

Beck, Andrew. "Natural Law and the Reformation." *The Clergy Review* 21 (1941): 73–81.

Bennett, Arthur. The Valley of Vision : A Collection of Puritan Prayers and Devotions. Edinburgh: Banner of Truth Trust, 2009.

Berns, Walter. "John Milton 1608-1674." *History of Political Philosophy* (1972): 440–455.

Blackstone, Sir William. The Great Charter and Charter of the Forest. Clarendon Press, 1759.

Bodin, Jean, and M. J. Tooley. *Six Books of the Commonwealth*. Vol. 56. B. Blackwell Oxford, 1955.

Boogman, Johan Christiaan. "The Union of Utrecht. Its Genesis and Consequences." *BMGN-Low Countries Historical Review* 94, no. 3 (1979): 377–407.

Bossuet, Jacques Bénigne, and Jean Siffrein Maury. Sermons choisis de Bossuet : suivis d'extraits de ses divers sermons, et précédés du discours préliminaire sur les sermons de Bossuet. Paris: Firmin-Didot, 1845.

Bostock, David. "Aristotle's Ethics" (2000).

Bowman, George Ernest. The Mayflower Compact and Its Signers: With Facsimiles and a List of the Mayflower Passengers. Massachusetts society of Mayflower descendants, 1920.

Boyer, Allen D. Sir Edward Coke and the Elizabethan Age. Stanford University Press, 2003.

Brauer, Jerald C. "Types of Puritan Piety." Church History 56, no. 1 (1987): 39–58.

Brentano, Robert. Robert Winchelsey and the Crown, 1294-1313. A Study in the Defence of Ecclesiastical Liberty. JSTOR, 1982.

Burke, Edmund. A Philosophical Enquiry Into the Origin of Our Ideas of the Sublime and Beautiful. Wentworth Press, 2016.

Burke, Edmund. Speech of Edmund Burke, Esq., on American Taxation, April 19, 1774. [Place of publication not identified]: Hardpress Publishing, 2012.

Burke, Edmund, W. M. Elofson, Paul. Langford, and John A. Woods. The Writings and Speeches of Edmund Burke. Oxford: Clarendon Press, 1996.

Burke, Edmund., and Leslie G. Mitchell. Reflections on the Revolution in France. Oxford: Oxford Univ. Press, 2009.

Cameron, J. K. "The Piety of Samuel Rutherford (C. 1621-1661): A Neglected Feature of Seventeenth Century Scottish Calvinism." Nederlands archief voor kerkgeschiedenis / Dutch Review of Church History 65, no. 1/2 (1985): 153–159. http://www.jstor.org/stable/24012447.

Campbell, William M. "Lex, Rex and Its Author." Records of the Scottish Church History Society 7, no. 3 (1941).

Carpenter, D. A. "Simon de Montfort: The First Leader of a Political Movement in English History." History 76, no. 246 (1991): 3–23.

Chafee, Zechariah. Documents on Fundamental Human Rights: The Anglo-American Tradition. Vol. 1. Atheneum, 1963.

Chisholm, Hugh. "King and Divine Right of Kings." Encyclopædia Britannica. Cambridge: Cambridge University Press, 1911.

Co, Aero Mayflower Transit, and William Bradford. The Mayflower Compact. The Company, 1955.

Coffey, John, ed. "Conclusion:" In *John Goodwin and the Puritan Revolution*, 291–297. Boydell and Brewer, 2006. http://www.jstor.org/stable/10.7722/j.ctt81kbk.16.

———. Politics, Religion and the British Revolutions: The Mind of Samuel Rutherford. Cambridge University Press, 1997.

Coldwell, Chris, and Matthew Winzer. "The Westminster Assembly and the Judicial Law: A Chronoligal Compilation and Analysis, Part 1: Chronology." *The Confessional Presbyterian* 5 (2009): 3–55.

Coldwell, Christopher, and Matthew Winzer. "The Westminster Assembly & the Judicial Law: A Chronological Compilation and Analysis." *The Confessional Presbyterian* 5 (2009): 3. http://search.ebscohost.com/login.aspx?direct=true&db=lsdar&AN=ATLA0001764455&site=ehost-live.

Cooper, James. "Sprott George Washington." Edited by Sidney Lee. *Dictionary of National Biography, 1912 Supplement*. London: Smith, Elder & Co., 1912. Wikisource.

Corbett, R. J. *Lockean Commonwealth, The*. State University of New York Press, 2010. https://books.google.com/books?id=VTKbZ74tsYgC.

Corns, Thomas N., ed. *The Cambridge Companion to English Poetry, Donne to Marvell*. Cambridge Companions to Literature. Cambridge: Cambridge University Press, 1993. https://www.cambridge.org/core/books/cambridge-companion-to-english-poetry-donne-to-marvell/18F10777F88F7EC3DFDEC25C4C8B87BA.

Culberson, James Kevin. "'For Reformation and Uniformity': George Gillespie (1613--1648) and the Scottish Covenanter Revolution." (2004).

Danner, Dan Gordon. "The Theology of the Geneva Bible of 1560: A Study in English Protestantism.," 1969.

De Freitas, S. A., and A. W. G. Raath. "Samuel Rutherford and the Soteriological Implications of the Office of Magistracy in the Covenanted Christian Community." *Journal for Christian Scholarship = Tydskrif vir Christelike Wetenskap* 43, no. 3_4 (2007): 31–50.

De Freitas, Shaun. "A Reply to John Coffey's Analysis of Samuel Rutherford's Theology and Political Theory." *journal for christian scholarship* 51 (January 1, 2015): 69.

De Freitas, Shaun Alberto. "Law and Federal-Republicanism: Samuel Rutherford's Quest for a Constitutional Model." University of the Free State, 2014.

De Freitas, Shaun, and Andries Raath. "Samuel Rutherford and the Neo-Thomists : juristic corporation theory and natural law arguments in Lex, Rex." *Journal for Christian Scholarship = Tydskrif vir Christelike Wetenskap* 51, no. 2 (2015): 27–53.

De Freitas, Shaun Alberto, and A. W. G. Raath. "Samuel Rutherford and the Protection of Religious Freedom in Early Seventeenth-Century Scotland" (2016).

De Vitoria, Francisco. Francisci de Victoria De Indis et De Ivre Belli Relectiones: Being Parts of Relectiones Theologicae XII by Franciscus de Victoria. Carnegie Institution of Washington, 1917.

Dick, J. *Lectures on Theology*. Robert Carter, 1851. https://books.google.com/books?id=WX5CAAAAIAAJ.

Donne, John. *Devotions upon Emergent Occasions*. Oxford University Press on Demand, 1987.

Donne, John, T. W. Craik, and R. J. Craik. *John Donne : Selected Poetry and Prose*. London; New York: Methuen, 1986.

Dreisbach, Daniel L., and Mark David Hall. Faith and the Founders of the American Republic. Oxford University Press, 2014.

van Dyke, Vernen. "Sphere Sovereignty of Religious Institutions: A Contemporary Calvinistic Theory of Church-State Relations" (2001).

Edwards, J. Goronwy. "Confirmatio Cartarum and Baronial Grievances in 1297." *The English Historical Review* 58, no. 230 (1943): 147–171.

Edwards, Lee. Just Right : A Life in Pursuit of Liberty, 2017.

Elazar, Daniel. Covenant and Commonwealth. Routledge, 2018.

Emon, Anver. "Reflections on the Constitution of Medina: An Essay on Methodology and Ideology in Islamic Legal History." *UCLA J. Islamic & Near EL* 1 (2001): 103.

FATOVIC, CLEMENT, ed. "CONSTRUCTING THE CONSTITUTION:" In *America's Founding and the Struggle over Economic Inequality*, 126–190.

University Press of Kansas, 2015. http://www.jstor.org/stable/j.ctt1qft3b0.9.

Federici, Michael P. "Eric Voegelin : The Restoration of Order." Last modified 2002. http://books.google.com/books?id=5N-FAAAAMAAJ.

Ferguson, Niall. Civilization : *The West and the Rest*. London: Allen Lane, 2011.

Finnis, John. *Natural Law and Natural Rights*. Oxford University Press, 2011.

Fisher, E., and T. Boston. *The Marrow of Modern Divinity: In Two Parts ...* W. Paxton, 1830. https://books.google.com/books?id=LwI3AAAAMAAJ.

Flinn, Richard. "1979,'Samuel Rutherford and Puritan Political Theory.'" *The Journal for Christian Reconstruction* 5, no. 2 (1978): 49–74.

Fossedal, Gregory. Direct Democracy in Switzerland. Routledge, 2018.

Frederick II, Holy Roman Emperor, and James M. Powell. The Liber Augustalis: Or, Constitutions of Melfi, Promulgated by the Emperor Frederick II for the Kingdom of Sicily in 1231. Syracuse, NY]: Syracuse University Press, 1971.

Fuller, Thomas. Works, Including History of the Church in Britain. Third. London: Tegg, 1840.

Garver, S. Joel. "Liberty of Conscience in Catholic, Reformed, and Contemporary Perspective." *Joelgarver.com* 10 (2005).

Gatis, George J. "Puritan Jurisprudence: A Study in Substantive Biblical Law." *Contra Mundum* 12 (1994): 1–15.

George, Robert P. Conscience and Its Enemies : Confronting the Dogmas of Liberal Secularism, 2016.

Gillespie, G. *The Presbyterian's Armoury: Lex, Rex, or The Law and the Prince*. R. Ogle and Oliver & Boyd, 1846. https://books.google.com/books?id=EgRMAAAAYAAJ.

Gilmour, Robert. Samuel Rutherford: A Study: Biographical and Somewhat Critical, in the History of the Scottish Covenant. Oliphant, Anderson & Ferrier, 1904.

Gottlieb, Paula. "The Virtue of Aristotle's Ethics" (2009).

Gragg, Rod. "By the Hand of Providence : How Faith Shaped the

American Revolution." Last modified 2014. https://www.overdrive.com/search?q=129857EC-03A8-405F-8078-3E8819B0AE1C.

———. "Forged in Faith : How Faith Shaped the Birth of the Nation 1607-1776." Last modified 2014. https://www.overdrive.com/search?q=EAD46C2D-9D72-4A5C-A945-A74E970388DB.

Gribben, Crawford. "Samuel Rutherford and Liberty of Conscience." *Westminster Theological Journal* 71, no. 2 (2009): 355–373.

Grosby, Steven. "Jerusalem and Athens: In Defense of Jerusalem." *Hebraic Political Studies* 3, no. 3 (2008): 239–60.

Grotius, Hugo. "The Law of War and Peace, Trans." *FW Kelsey, Bobbs-Merrill, Indianapolis, IN* (1925).

Guardini, Romano. *The End of the Modern World*. Wilmington, Delaware: ISI Books, 2013.

Halecki, Kathleen. "Scottish Ministers, Covenant Theology, and the Idea of the Nation, 1560-1638." Union Institute and University, 2012.

Hall, D. W. *The Genevan Reformation and the American Founding*. Lexington Books, 2005. https://books.google.co.uk/books?id=jmdP3ZS3lfAC.

Hall, David W. *Election Day Sermons*. Oak Ridge, TN: Kuyper Institute, 1996.

———. *Paradigms in Polity*. William B. Eerdmans Publishing Company, 1994.

———. Savior or Servant?: Putting Government in Its Place. Kuyper Institute, 1996.

Hall, P. The Harmony of Protestant Confessions: Exhibiting the Faith of the Churches of Christ ... J.F. Shaw, 1842. https://books.google.com/books?id=Xv8QAAAAIAAJ.

Hardie, William Francis Ross. "Aristotle's Ethical Theory" (1980).

Harman, Allan M. "Francis Schaeffer and the Shaping of Evangelical America." *The Reformed Theological Review* 72, no. 1 (April 2013): 65–67. http://search.ebscohost.com/login.aspx?direct=true&db=lsdar&AN=ATLA0001955480&site=ehost-live.

Haxtun, Annie Arnoux. *Signers of the Mayflower Compact*. Vol. 2. Reprinted from the Mail and express, 1897.

Herz, Peter J. "Covenant to Constitutionalism: Rule of Law as a Theological Ideal in Reformed Scotland." (2003).

Hobbes, Thomas, and Sterling P. Lamprecht. "De Cive or The Citizen" (1949).

Hodge, C. *The Biblical Repertory and Princeton Review*. James A. Peabody, 1840. https://books.google.com/books?id=UlQAAAAAYAAJ.

———. The Reunion Of The Old And New-School Presbyterian Churches, 1867. https://books.google.com/books?id=6BGceH6DBEgC.

Howie, John. Lives of the Scottish Covenanters : Being a Brief Historical Account of the Most Eminent Noblemen, Gentlemen, Ministers, and Others, Who Testified or Suffered for the Cause of Reformation in Scotland, from the Beginning of the Sixteenth Century to the Year 1688. Glasgow: McPhun, 1863.

Hunt, L. A. *Inventing Human Rights: A History*. W.W. Norton & Company, 2007. https://books.google.com/books?id=oSJJJsdG--kC.

Hurnard, Naomi D. "The Jury of Presentment and the Assize of Clarendon." *English Historical Review* (1941): 374–410.

Hutchinson, Douglas S. The Virtues of Aristotle. Routledge, 2015.

Hutson, James H. Forgotten Features of the Founding: The Recovery of Religious Themes in the Early American Republic. Lexington Books, 2003.

Jacobs, Patrick Joseph Dominic. "The Influence of Biblical Ideas and Principles on Early American Republicanism and History" (1999).

Jenks, Edward. "The Prerogative Writs in English Law." *The Yale Law Journal* 32, no. 6 (1923): 523–534.

Kelly, D. F. The Emergence of Liberty in the Modern World: The Influence of Calvin on Five Governments from the 16th Through 18th Centuries. P&R Pub., 1992. https://books.google.com/books?id=roZSNAAACAAJ.

Kilcullen, John. "The Origin of Property: Ockham, Grotius, Pufendorf, and Some Others" (1995).

Kim, San-Deog. "Time and Eternity: A Study in Samuel Rutherford's Theology, with Reference to His Use of Scholastic Method." University of Aberdeen, 2002.

Kirk, Russell. "The Roots of American Order." Last modified 2014. http://search.ebscohost.com/login. aspx?direct=true&scope=site&db=nlebk&db=nlabk&AN=1059690.

Klarer, M. *A Short Literary History of the United States.* Taylor & Francis, 2014. https://books.google.com/books?id=rLauAwAAQBAJ.

Kopel, D. B. The Morality of Self-Defense and Military Action: The Judeo-Christian Tradition. ABC-CLIO, 2017. https://books.google.com/books?id=QN4jDgAAQBAJ.

Kopel, David. "The Scottish and English Religious Roots of the American Right to Arms: Buchanan, Rutherford, Locke, Sidney, and the Duty to Overthrow Tyranny" (2005).

de La Boétie, Étienne. Discourse on Voluntary Servitude. Hackett Publishing, 2012.

Languet, Hubert, and Stephanius Jurius Brutus. Brutus: Vindiciae, Contra Tyrannos: Or, Concerning the Legitimate Power of a Prince Over the People, and of the People Over a Prince. Cambridge University Press, 1994.

Lecky, W. E. H. History of the Rise and Influence of Rationalism in Europe, Vol. II. London: Longmans, Green and Co, 1866.

Locke, John. Second Treatise of Government: An Essay Concerning the True Original, Extent and End of Civil Government. John Wiley & Sons, 2014.

———. *Two Treatises of Government.* for Whitmore and Fenn, and C. Brown, 1821.

Locke, John, and Edmund Law. *The Works of John Locke,.* London: Printed for W. Strahan, 1777.

Lutz, Donald S. "Religious Dimensions in the Development of American Constitutionalism." *Emory LJ* 39 (1990): 21.

———. "The Mayflower Compact, 1620." The Roots of the Republic: American Founding Documents Interpreted (1990): 17–23.

Machiavelli, Niccolò. "Discourses on Livy, Trans. Harvey C. Mansfield and Nathan Tarcov." *Chicago: University of Chicago Press* 2 (1996): 5.

Machiavelli, Niccolo. "The Prince and Discourses On the First Decade of Titus Livius." *New York: The Modern Library* (1940).

Maclear, J. F. "Samuel Rutherford: The Law and the King." *Calvinism and the political order* (1965): 65–87.

Marshall, John Lewis. "Natural Law and the Covenant: The Place of Natural Law in the Covenantal Framework of Samuel Rutherford's Lex, Rex." Westminster Theological Seminary, Philadelphia, 1995.

Mason, Alpheus Thomas. Free Government in the Making; Readings in American Political Thought. New York: Oxford University Press, 1965.

Mather, C., and T. Robbins. Magnalia Christi Americana: Or, The Ecclesiastical History of New-England, from Its First Planting, in the Year 1620, Unto the Year of Our Lord 1698 ... S. Andrus & son, 1853. https://books.google.com/books?id=f0Y5s7bsqDQC.

Maxwell, John. *Sacro-Sancta Regum Majestas: Or The Sacred and Royal Prerogative of Christian Kings*. London (original); Ann Arbor, MI; Oxford (UK): printed for Tho. Dring, over against the Inner-Temple-Gate in Fleet-street; digital edition by Text Creation Partnership, 1680. https://quod.lib.umich.edu/e/eebo/A50351.0001.001?view=toc.

McAnnally-Linz, Ryan. "Resistance and Romans 13 in Samuel Rutherford's Lex, Rex." *Scottish Journal of Theology* 66, no. 2 (2013): 140–158.

McGrath, Alister E. The Intellectual Origins of the European Reformation. John Wiley & Sons, 2008.

McIlroy, David H. "How Is the Rule of Law a Limit on Power?" *Studies in Christian Ethics* 29, no. 1 (February 2016): 34–50. http://search.ebscohost.com/login.aspx?direct=true&db=lsdar&AN=ATLAn3841850&site=ehost-live.

McKechnie, William Sharp. Magna Carta: A Commentary on the Great Charter of King John. J. Maclehose and sons, 1914.

McLaren, Anne. "Reading Sir Thomas Smith's De Republica Anglorum as Protestant Apologetic." *The Historical Journal* 42, no. 4 (1999): 911–939.

Miller, Fred. "Aristotle's Political Theory" (1998).

Miller, Fred Dycus. Nature, Justice, and Rights in Aristotle's Politics. Oxford University Press, 1997.

Miller, Jon. *The Reception of Aristotle's Ethics*. Cambridge University Press, 2012.

Miller, Perry, and H. JOHNSON. The Puritans. A Sourcebook of Their Writings. 2 Vols. Bound as One. New York: Dover Publications Inc, 2001.

Milton, Michael Anthony. "The Application of the Theology of the Westminster Assembly in the Ministry of the Welsh Puritan Vavasor Powell (1617-1670)." University of Wales Lampeter, 1997.

Mitchell, Alexander F. The Westminster Assembly: Its History and Standards. Puritan Publications, 2012.

Moots, G. A. Politics Reformed: The Anglo-American Legacy of Covenant Theology. University of Missouri Press, 2010. https://books.google.com/books?id=IJCcK2VDB3wC.

Moots, Glenn Andrew. "The Evolution of Reformed Political Thought and the Revival of Natural Law Theory." Louisiana State University, Baton Rouge, 1993.

More, Thomas. Utopia, Eds George M. Logan & Robert M. Adams. Cambridge University Press, Cambridge UK, 1989.

Mullan, David George. "Mystic and Scholastic." Edited by John Coffey. The Review of Politics 62, no. 1 (2000): 137–139. http://www.jstor.org/stable/1408154.

Mulligan, Robert F. "The Common Law Character of English Charters: Spontaneous Order in the Constitutions of Clarendon (1164)." Constitutional Political Economy 16, no. 3 (2005): 285–311.

Nellen, Henk. "Minimal Religion, Deism and Socinianism: On Grotius's Motives for Writing De Veritate." Grotiana 33, no. 1 (2012): 25–57.

Obama, Barrack H. "President Barack Obama's State of the Union Address." Whitehouse.Gov. Last modified January 28, 2014. Accessed March 21, 2018. https://obamawhitehouse.archives.gov/the-press-office/2014/01/28/president-barack-obamas-state-union-address.

O'Donovan, Joan Lockwood. "Political Authority and European Community: The Challenge of the Christian Political Tradition." Scottish journal of theology 47, no. 1 (1994): 1–18.

Old South Church (Boston, Mass). The Form of Covenant, of the Old South Church in Boston, Massachusetts, with Lists of the Founders, the Pastors, the Ruling Elders and Deacons, and the Members. Crocker & Brewster, 1833.

https://books.google.com/books?id=lO7h5NHMQpAC.

Ormond, D. D. *A Kirk and a College in the Craigs of Stirling*. Stirling [Scotland]: Journal and Advertiser Office, 1897.

Packer, J. I. A *Quest for Godliness: The Puritan Vision of the Christian Life*. Crossway Books, 1994. https://books.google.com/books?id=FxGiTGxd_M0C.

Paganelli, Maria Pia. "Recent Engagements with Adam Smith and the Scottish Enlightenment." *History of Political Economy* 47, no. 3 (2015): 363–394.

Paine, Thomas. The Political Works of Thomas Paine : Complete in One Volume : Now First Collected Together, and to Which Are Added Several Pieces Never before Published in England ; and an Appendix, Containing the Trial of Thomas Paine at Guildhall. London: W. Dugdale, 1844.

Paul, Robert S. (Robert Sydney). "Political Ideas of the English Civil Wars, 1641-1649: A Collection of Representative Texts with a Commentary." *Church History* 55, no. 2 (June 1986): 254–254. http://search.ebscohost.com/login.aspx?direct=true&db=lsdar&AN=ATLA0000542748&site=ehost-live.

Perry, Richard L. Sources of Our Liberties. McGraw-Hill, 1964.

———. Sources of Our Liberties. McGraw-Hill, 1964.

———. Sources of Our Liberties: Documentary Origins of Individual Liberties in the United States Constitution and Bill of Rights. American Bar Foundation, 1978.

Raath, A. W. G. "Moral Duty, Natural Rights and the Ciceronian Impact on the Political Views of Luther and Calvin." *Journal for Christian Scholarship= Tydskrif vir Christelike Wetenskap* 49, no. 4 (2013): 1–26.

Raath, A. W. G., and S. A. De Freitas. "John Milton's Federal-Republicanism." *Journal for Christian Scholarship= Tydskrif vir Christelike Wetenskap* 44, no. 3_4 (2008): 179–202.

Raath, Andries. "Providence, Conscience of Liberty and Benevolence-the Implications of Luther's and Calvin's Views on Natural Law for Fundamental Rights." *In die Skriflig* 41, no. 3 (2007): 415–442.

———. "The Transformation of Reformed Natural Law Doctrine in Samuel Rutherford's Lex, Rex." *Koers - Bulletin for Christian Scholarship* 80, no. 4 (December 15, 2015). Accessed April 4, 2018. http://www.koersjournal.org.

za/index.php/koers/article/view/2245.

———. "The transformation of reformed natural law doctrine in Samuel Rutherford's Lex, Rex : original research." *Koers : Bulletin for Christian Scholarship = Koers : Bulletin vir Christelike Wetenskap* 80, no. 4 (2015): 1–10.

Raath, Andries, and Shaun De Freitas. "Samuel Rutherford's Theologico-Political Federalism in Early American Society." *Journal for Christian Scholarship= Tydskrif vir Christelike Wetenskap* 48, no. 3_4 (2012): 1–42.

———. "Theologically United and Divided: The Political Covenantalism of Samuel Rutherford and John Milton." *The Westminster theological journal* 67, no. 2 (2005): 301–321.

Raath, A.W.G. "Samuel Rutherford's contribution to Reformed republicanism." *Journal for Christian Scholarship = Tydskrif vir Christelike Wetenskap* 51, no. 1 (2015): 93–115.

Raath, A.W.G., and S.A. De Freitas. "From Luther to the founding fathers : Puritanism and the Ciceronian spirit on natural law, covenant, and resistance to tyranny." *Journal for Christian Scholarship = Tydskrif vir Christelike Wetenskap* 43, no. 3_4 (2007): 157–177.

Rakove, Jack N. *The Annotated U.S. Constitution and Declaration of Independence*. Reprint edition. Cambridge, Mass.; London: Belknap Press, 2012.

Rendell, Kingsley G. Samuel Rutherford: A New Biography of the Man & His Ministry. Christian Focus, 2003.

———. "Samuel Rutherford: The Man and His Ministry." Durham University, 1981.

Richard, G. M., and D. A. S. Fergusson. *The Supremacy of God in the Theology of Samuel Rutherford*. Wipf & Stock Publishers, 2009. https://books.google.com/books?id=fQhMAwAAQBAJ.

Richards, Peter Judson. "'The Law Written in Their Hearts'?: Rutherford and Locke on Nature, Government and Resistance." *Journal of Law and Religion* 18, no. 1 (2002): 151–189. http://www.jstor.org/stable/1051497.

Robinson, Jonathan. William of Ockham's Early Theory of Property Rights in Context. Vol. 166. Brill, 2012.

Rorty, Amélie. *Essays on Aristotle's Rhetoric*. Vol. 6. Univ of California Press, 1996.

Ross, David, and William David Ross. Aristotelis Politica; Recognovit Brevique Adnotatione Critica Instruxit WD Ross. Clarendon Press, 1957.

Rouse, Richard H., and Mary A. Rouse. "John of Salisbury and the Doctrine of Tyrannicide." *Speculum* 42, no. 4 (1967): 693–709.

Rutherford, S. Lex, Rex, Or, The Law and the Prince: A Dispute for the Just Prerogative of King and People, Containing the Reasons and Causes of the Most Necessary Defensive Wars of the Kingdom of Scotland and of Their Expedition for the Aid and Help of Their Dear Brethren of England. In Which Their Innocency Is Asserted and a Full Answer Is Given to a Seditious Pamphlet Entituled, "Sacro-Sancta Regum Majestas," Or, The Sacred and Royal Prerogative of Christian Kings ; Under the Name of J.A., But Penned by John Maxwell ... Robert Ogle and Oliver & Boyd, 1843. https://books.google.com/books?id=5LYxAQAAMAAJ.

———. *The Loveliness of Christ*. Banner of Truth Trust, 2007. https://books.google.com/books?id=5IvmPQAACAAJ.

Rutherford, S., and H. Smith. *Extracts from the Letters of Samuel Rutherford*. Scripture Truth Publications, 2008. https://books.google.com/books?id=-23TglJAZNwC.

Rutherford, Samuel. A Survey of the Spirituall Antichrist : Opening the Secrets of Familisme and Antinomianisme in the Antichristian Doctrine of John Saltmarsh, and Will. Del, the Present Preachers of the Army Now in England, and of Robert Town, Tob. Crisp, H. Denne, Eaton, and Others ... London: Printed by J.D. & R.I. for Andrew Crooke, 1648.

RUTHERFORD, SAMUEL. LETTERS OF SAMUEL RUTHERFORD, : With Biographical Sketches of His Correspondents;... with a Sketch of His Life (Classic Reprint). [S.l.]: FORGOTTEN BOOKS, 2017.

Rutherford, Samuel. *Letters of Samuel Rutherford (Third Edition)*. Edited by Andrew A. (Andrew Alexander) Bonar, 2013. Accessed May 1, 2018. http://www.gutenberg.org/ebooks/42557?msg=welcome_stranger.

———. Lex, Rex, Or, The Law and the Prince: In Fourty-Four Questions. Sprinkle Publications, 1982.

―――. Lex, Rex : The Law and the Prince. A Dispute for the Just Prerogative of King and People. Containing the Reasons and Causes of the Most Necessary Defensive Wars of the Kingdom of Scotland, and of Their Expedition for the Ayd and Help of Their Dear Brethren of England. In Which Their Innocency Is Asserted, and a Full Answer Is given to a Seditious Pamphlet, Intituled, Sacro-Sancta Regum Majestas, or The Sacred and Royall Prerogative of Christian Kings; under the Name of J.A. But Penned by Jo: Maxwell the Excommunicate ⸗. Prelat. With a Scripturall Confutation of the Ruinous Grounds of W. Barclay, H. Grotius, H. Arnisoeus, Ant. de Domi. P. Bishop of Spalata, and of Other Late Anti-Magistratical Royalists; as, the Author of Ossorianum, D. Fern, E. Symmons, the Doctors of Aberdeen, &c. In XLIV. Questions. Published by Authority. London: Printed for Iohn Field, and are to be sold at his house upon Addle-hill, neer Baynards-Castle, 1644.

―――. The Due Right of Presbyteries. John Field, n.d.

―――. The Prison Sayings of Samuel Rutherford ... 1637. With an Introductory Sketch of His Character. London, 1854.

Rutherford, Samuel, and Banner of Truth Trust. *The Trial and Triumph of Faith*. Edinburgh; Carlisle, PA: Banner of Truth Trust, 2001.

Rutherford, Samuel, and John Gordon Kenmure. *Conversations with a Dying Man*, 2017.

Rutherford, Samuel, and Ellen S. Lister. *The Loveliness of Christ*. London: S. Bagster, 1958.

Sandoz, Ellis. A Government of Laws: Political Theory, Religion, and the American Founding. Vol. 1. University of Missouri Press, 2001.

Sandoz, Ellis. Political Sermons of the American Founding Era 1730-1805. Indianapolis: Liberty Fund Inc., 2014.

Sandoz, Ellis. "Religion and the American Founding." *Regent UL Rev.* 20 (2007): 17.

Schaeffer, Francis A. "The God Who Is There (1968) in The Complete Works of Francis A. Schaeffer A Christian Worldview, 5 Vols." *Wheaton, IL: Crossway Books* 1 (1982): 7.

Schaff, P. *The Creeds of Christendom: With a History and Critical Notes, Vol III*. Harper & Brothers, 1584. https://books.google.com/

books?id=7gMNAAAAIAAJ.

Scotland, Church of. The Confession of Faith: The Larger and Shorter Catechisms, with the Scripture-Proofs at Large, Together with the Sum of Saving Knowledge, (Contained in the Holy Scriptures, and Held Forth in the Said Confession and Catechisms,) and Practical Use Thereof : Covenants, National and Solemn League; Acknowledgement of Sins, and Engagement to Duties, Directories for Public and Family Worship; Form of Church Government, &c., of Publick Authority in the Church of Scotland; with Acts of Assembly and Parliament, Relative To, and Approbative Of, the Same. D. Hunter Blair and M.S. Tyndall Bruce, 1845. https://books.google.com/books?id=L2cXAAAAYAAJ.

Scotland, Church of, and Associate Reformed Presbyterian Church. The Confession of Faith, the Larger and Shorter Catechisms, with the Scripture-Proofs at Large: The Covenants, National and Solemn League, the Acknowledgment of Sins, and Engagement to Duties. The Directories for Public, and Family Worship. Together with The Sum of Saving Knowledge (Contained in the Holy Scriptures, and Held Forth in the Said Confession and Catechisms) and Practical Use Thereof. And the Form of Church Government, with Acts of Assembly and Parliament Relative To, and Approbative Of, the Same. W.W. Woodward, 1813. https://books.google.com/books?id=fCoPAAAAIAAJ.

Scott, Samuel Parsons. The Civil Law: Including the Twelve Tables, the Institutes of Gaius, the Rules of Ulpian, the Opinions of Paulus, the Enactments of Justinian, and the Constitutions of Leo. Vol. 1. The Lawbook Exchange, Ltd., 2001.

———. The Visigothic Code:(Forum Judicum). Boston Book Company, 1910.

Scott, T. The Articles of the Synod of Dort, and Its Rejection of Errors: With the History of Events Which Made Way for That Synod, as Published by the Authority of the States-General; and the Documents Confirming Its Decisions. W. Williams, 1831. https://books.google.com/books?id=OfBMYEOMHCEC.

Shaw, R. *An Exposition of the Confession of Faith of the Westminister Assembly of Divines.* Presbyterian board of publication, 1847. https://books.google.com/books?id=ZUUXAAAAYAAJ.

Simpson, Grant G. "The Declaration of Arbroath Revitalised." *The Scottish Historical Review* 56, no. 161 (1977): 11–33.

Simpson, Peter L. Phillips. *A Philosophical Commentary on the Politics of Aristotle*. Chapel Hill, N.C.: University of North Carolina Press, 2002.

Smart, Ian M. "Liberty and Authority: The Political Ideas of Presbyterians in England and Scotland during the Seventeenth Century." University of Strathclyde, 1978.

Smart, Ian Michael. "THE POLITICAL IDEAS OF THE SCOTTISH COVENANTERS. 1638–88." *History of Political Thought* 1, no. 2 (1980): 167–193. http://www.jstor.org/stable/26211777.

Smith, Adam. The Glasgow Edition of the Works and Correspondence of Adam Smith: VI: Correspondence. Vol. 6. Oxford University Press, 1987.

Smith, Thomas. De Republica Anglorum: A Discourse on the Commonwealth of England. The University Press, 1906.

Solzenicyn, Aleksandr I., and Edward E. Ericson. *The Solzhenitsyn Reader : New and Essential Writings, 1947-2005*. Wilmington, Del.: ISI Books, 2012.

Spade, Paul Vincent. *The Cambridge Companion to Ockham*. Cambridge University Press, 1999.

Spellman, W. M. *John Locke*. London: MacMillan Press, 1997.

Sprott, G. W. *WORSHIP & OFFICES OF THE CHURCH*. WENTWORTH Press, 2016. https://books.google.com/books?id=h7NVvgAACAAJ.

Sprott, George Washington. "Russen - Scobell." *Dictionary of National Biography*, 1885-1900, n.d. Wikisource.

———. "Rutherford Samuel." Edited by Sidney Lee. *Dictionary of National Biography, 1885-1900*. London: Elder Smith & Co., 1897. Wikisource.

Sprott, George Washington 1829-1909. The Worship and Offices of the Church of Scotland ...: Being Lectures Delivered at the Universities of Aberdeen, Glasgow, St. Andrews, and Edinburgh. Wentworth Press, 2016.

Stephen, Leslie. Dictionary of National Biography. New York: Macmillan, 1885.

Sutherland, Donald W. "Quo Warranto Proceedings in the Reign of Edward I,

1278-1294." University of Oxford, 1956.

Synod, Congregational churches in Massachusetts Cambridge, New England synod of elders and messengers of the churches, and Cambridge platform. *The Cambridge Platform of Church Discipline: Adopted in 1648; And, The Confession of Faith, Adopted in 1680*. Perkins & Whipple, 1850. https://books. google.com/books?id=_ZYEAAAAQAAJ.

Taylor, Charles. A Secular Age. Cambridge, Mass.: Belknap Press of Harvard University Press, 2007.

Taylor, Eustace Lovatt Hebden. "The Christian Philosophy of Law, Politics, and the State" (1966).

Taylor, F. Flagg. The Great Lie : Classic and Recent Appraisals of Ideology and Totalitarianism. Wilmington: ISI Books, 2011.

Thayer, James B. "Jury and Its Development." *Harv. L. Rev.* 5 (1891): 249.

Thompson, Faith. The First Century of Magna Carta: Why It Persisted as a Document. Russell & Russell, 1967.

Thomson, Andrew. *Samuel Rutherford*. Hodder and Stoughton, 1884.

Thornton, Bruce S. "A Student's Guide to Classics." Last modified 2003. http:// public.eblib.com/choice/publicfullrecord.aspx?p=1800241.

Todd, Lewis Paul, and Merle Eugene Curti. *Triumph of the American Nation*. Harcourt Brace Jovanovich, 1986.

Tuck, Richard. Natural Rights Theories: Their Origin and Development. Cambridge University Press, 1981.

United States Constitution Bicentennial Celebration (Philadelphia, Pa.). *Magna Carta*. Philadelphia, Pa.: U.S. Constitution Bicentennial Celebration, 1987.

U.S.A, Presbyterian Church in the. *The Constitution of the Presbyterian Church in the United States of America*. Presbyterian board of publication, 1839. https://books.google.com/books?id=kmcNAAAAYAAJ.

U.S.A, Presbyterian Church in the, and I. Watts. Parish Psalmody: A Collection of Psalms and Hymns for Public Worship: Containing Dr. Watts's Versification of the Psalms of David, Entire, a Large Portion of Dr. Watts's Hymns, and Psalms and Hymns by Other Authors, Selected and Original.

Perkins & Purves, 1844. https://books.google.com/books?id=tJ_ibeXR7YIC.

Usher, James. *A Body of Divinitie*, n.d. Accessed March 19, 2018. https://www.westminsterassembly.org/primary-source/a-body-of-divinitie/.

Van de Beek, A. "God's Omnipotence and Human Freedom." *Acta Theologica* 2002, no. Supplement 3 (2002): 169–186.

VAN DER STELT, John C. "Church in Society." *International Reo formed Bulletin* 11, no. 34 (1968): 15–36.

VanDrunen, D. Natural Law and the Two Kingdoms: A Study in the Development of Reformed Social Thought. Eerdmans Publishing Company, 2010. https://books.google.com/books?id=jnd9vRw51TwC.

Voegelin, Eric. *Order and History Vol.4, Vol.4,*. Baton Rouge: Lousiana State University, 1974.

Voegelin, Eric, and Dante Germino. *Order and History . Vol. 3, Vol. 3,*. Columbia; London: University Missouri Press, 2000.

Voegelin, Eric, and Athanasios Moulakis. *Order and History. Vol. II, Vol. II,*. Missouri: University of Missouri Press, 2000.

Volf, Miroslav. *A Public Faith · How Followers of Christ Should Serve the Common Good.* Brazos Press: Grand Rapids, Mich., 2011. http://ezproxy.sebts.edu/login?url=http://search.ebscohost.com/login.aspx?direct=true&scope=site&db=nlebk&db=nlabk&AN=530001.

Warbrick, Colin. "Freedom of Speech. By Barendt Eric.[Oxford: Clarendon Press. 1985. Xxiv+ 314 Pp.£ 35] The Tolerant Society: Freedom of Speech and Extremist Speech in America. By Bollinger Lee C..[New York: Cambridge University PressCambridge, UK. 1986. Vii+ 295 Pp.£ 18] Constitutional Opinions: Aspects of the Bill of Rights. By Levy Leonard W..[New York: Cambridge University PressCambridge, UK. 1986. Xi+ 272 Pp.£ 26• 50]." *International & Comparative Law Quarterly* 36, no. 2 (1987): 419–421.

Webb, Omri Kenneth. "The Political Thought of Samuel Rutherford." Duke University, 1964.

Webber, Joan. *Contrary Music. The Prose Style of John Donne.* Madison, University of Wisconsin Press, 1963.

Weber, M., and T. Parsons. *The Protestant Ethic and the Spirit of*

Capitalism. Dover Publications, 2003. https://books.google.com/books?id=fo9OIS7I0XAC.

Whittingham, William, John Hopkins, Michael H. Brown, and Thomas Sternhold. *The Geneva Bible : A Facsimile of the 1599 Edition with Undated Sternhold & Hopkins Psalms*. Ozark, Mo.: L.L. Brown Pub., 2003.

Wills, Garry. Inventing America: Jefferson's Declaration of Independence. Vintage, 2018.

Winthrop, John. "A Model of Christian Charity." *Winthrop Papers* 2 (1838): 1929–47.

Witte Jr, John. "The Freedom of a Christian: Martin Luther's Reformation of Law & Liberty" (2005).

Young, Cassie. "The Declaration of Arbroath" (2015).

Zaller, Robert. "The Figure of the Tyrant in English Revolutionary Thought." *Journal of the History of Ideas* 54, no. 4 (1993): 585–610.

Zeller, Eduard. Outlines of the History of Greek Philosophy. Routledge, 2014.

Zeller, Eduard, Benjamin Francis Conn Costelloe, and John Henry Muirhead. Aristotle and the Earlier Peripatetics: Being a Translation from Zeller's Philosophy of the Greeks. Vol. 2. London: Oxford University Press, 1897.

"A Pope and a President: John Paul II, Ronald Reagan, and the Extraordinary Untold Story of the 20th Century - Kindle Edition by Paul Kengor. Politics & Social Sciences Kindle EBooks @ Amazon.Com." Accessed April 7, 2018. https://www.amazon.com/Pope-President-Ronald-Extraordinary-Century-ebook/dp/B07BC771JK/ref=sr_1_1?s=books&ie=UTF8&qid=1523131415&sr=1-1&keywords=intercollegiate+studies+institute+books.

"Abolition of Star Chamber (1641)." *LONANG Institute*, n.d. Accessed April 7, 2018. https://lonang.com/library/organic/1641-asc/.

"Amazon.Com: Documents of American Constitutional and Legal History: Volume 1: From the Founding to 1896 (Documents of American Constitutional & Legal History) (9780195323115): Melvin I. Urofsky, Paul Finkelman: Books." Accessed October 20, 2018. https://www.amazon.com/Documents-American-Constitutional-Legal-History/dp/0195323114/ref=sr_1_fkmr0_1?ie=UTF8&qid=1540064095&sr=8-1-fkmr0&keywords=Sources+of+English+Constitutional+History%3A+600-1937%2C.

"America's Heritage - Constitutional Liberty." *LONANG Institute*, n.d. Accessed April 7, 2018. https://lonang.com/commentaries/conlaw/americas-heritage-constitutional-liberty/.

"BBC - History - Edmund Burke." Accessed April 4, 2018. http://www.bbc.co.uk/history/historic_figures/burke_edmund.shtml.

"Biblical Principles of Law - Herbert W. Titus." *LONANG Institute*, n.d. Accessed April 7, 2018. https://lonang.com/commentaries/curriculum/biblical-principles-of-law/.

"Bitesize Biographies: Samuel Rutherford." Servants of Grace. Last modified December 10, 2014. Accessed May 1, 2018. http://servantsofgrace.org/bitesize-biographies-samuel-rutherford/.

"Blaikie.SNPG.24.146 - Cathedral at St. Andrews - Jacobite Prints and Broadsides - National Library of Scotland." Accessed April 7, 2018. http://digital.nls.uk/jacobite-prints-and-broadsides/archive/75242285.

"Charter of Maryland (1632)." *LONANG Institute*, n.d. Accessed April 7, 2018. https://lonang.com/library/organic/1632-cm/.

"Charter of Massachusetts Bay (1629)." *LONANG Institute*, n.d. Accessed April 7, 2018. https://lonang.com/library/organic/1629-cmb/.

"Charter of Rhode Island (1663)." *LONANG Institute*, n.d. Accessed April 7, 2018. https://lonang.com/library/organic/1663-cri/.

"Church_history_of_Britain.Enw," n.d.

"Concessions and Agreements of West New Jersey (1677)." *LONANG Institute*, n.d. Accessed April 7, 2018. https://lonang.com/library/organic/1677-cnj/.

"Confirmatio Cartarum (1297)." LONANG Institute, n.d. Accessed April 7, 2018. https://lonang.com/library/organic/1297-cc/.

"CPJ5-JudiciallawtableWA.Pdf," n.d. Accessed April 4, 2018. https://www.cpjournal.com/wp-content/uploads/2016/12/CPJ5-judiciallawtableWA.pdf.

"Declaration and Resolves of the First Continental Congress (1774)." LONANG Institute, n.d. Accessed April 7, 2018. https://lonang.com/library/organic/1774-fcc/.

"Declaration of Causes and Necessity of Taking Up Arms (1775)."

LONANG Institute, n.d. Accessed April 7, 2018. https://lonang.com/library/organic/1775-dcn/.

"Declaration of Independence (1776)." *LONANG Institute*, n.d. Accessed April 7, 2018. https://lonang.com/library/organic/1776-di/.

"Delaware Declaration of Rights (1776)." *LONANG Institute*, n.d. Accessed April 7, 2018. https://lonang.com/library/organic/1776-ddr/.

"Edmund Burke & the Duties of Generations." *The Imaginative Conservative*, September 12, 2016. Accessed April 12, 2018. http://www.theimaginativeconservative.org/2016/09/edmund-burke-and-duties-generations-bradley-birzer.html.

"English Bill of Rights (1689)." *LONANG Institute*, n.d. Accessed April 7, 2018. https://lonang.com/library/organic/1689-br/.

"First Charter of Virginia (1606)." *LONANG Institute*, n.d. Accessed April 7, 2018. https://lonang.com/library/organic/1606-fcv/.

"Frame of Government of Pennsylvania (1682)." *LONANG Institute*, n.d. Accessed April 7, 2018. https://lonang.com/library/organic/1682-fgp/.

"Fundamental Orders of Connecticut (1639)." *LONANG Institute*, n.d. Accessed April 7, 2018. https://lonang.com/library/organic/1639-foc/.

"Great Britain Treaty (Act) of Union, 1707." *LONANG Institute*, n.d. Accessed April 7, 2018. https://lonang.com/library/organic/1707-tou/.

"Habeas Corpus Act (1679)." *LONANG Institute*, n.d. Accessed April 7, 2018. https://lonang.com/library/organic/1679-hca/.

"How Samuel Rutherford Changed My Life." *5 Minutes in Church History*. Last modified May 18, 2016. Accessed May 1, 2018. https://www.5minutesinchurchhistory.com/how-samuel-rutherford-changed-my-life/.

"John C. Calhoun: Political Writings." Accessed October 20, 2018. http://www.constitution.org/jcc/jcc.htm.

"Last Speeches of Kenmure (Free PDF Download)." Accessed May 1, 2018. http://www.portagepub.com/products/caa/sr-kenmure.html.

"Magna Carta (1215)." *LONANG Institute*, n.d. Accessed April 7, 2018. https://lonang.com/library/organic/1215-mc/.

"Maryland Declaration of Rights (1776)." *LONANG Institute*, n.d. Accessed April 7, 2018. https://lonang.com/library/organic/1776-mdr/.

"Massachusetts Body of Liberties (1641)." *LONANG Institute*, n.d. Accessed April 7, 2018. https://lonang.com/library/organic/1641-mbl/.

"Massachusetts Declaration of Rights (1780)." *LONANG Institute*, n.d. Accessed April 7, 2013. https://lonang.com/library/organic/1780-mdr/.

"Mayflower Compact (1620)." *LONANG Institute*, n.d. Accessed April 7, 2018. https://lonang.com/library/organic/1620-mc/.

"New Hampshire Bill of Rights (1784)." *LONANG Institute*, n.d. Accessed April 7, 2018. https://lonang.com/library/organic/1784-nhr/.

"Northwest Ordinance (1787)." *LONANG Institute*, n.d. Accessed April 7, 2018. https://lonang.com/library/organic/1787-no/.

"Ordinances for Virginia (1621)." *LONANG Institute*, n.d. Accessed April 7, 2018. https://lonang.com/library/organic/1621-ov/.

"Pamphlets in American History: GROUP I A Bibliographic Guide to the Microform Collection Edited by Henry Barnard," n.d. Accessed April 7, 2018. http://media2.proquest.com/documents/PAH_group_I.pdf.

"Pennsylvania Charter of Privileges (1701)." *LONANG Institute*, n.d. Accessed April 7, 2018. https://lonang.com/library/organic/1701-pcp/.

"Pennsylvania Declaration of Rights (1776)." *LONANG Institute*, n.d. Accessed April 7, 2018. https://lonang.com/library/organic/1776-pdr/.

"Petition of Right (1628)." *LONANG Institute*, n.d. Accessed April 7, 2018. https://lonang.com/library/organic/1628-pr/.

"Reflecting on Edmund Burke's 'Reflections.'" *The Imaginative Conservative*, March 13, 2018. Accessed April 12, 2018. http://www.theimaginativeconservative.org/2018/03/edmund-burke-reflections-bradley-birzer.html.

"Resolutions of the Stamp Act Congress (1765)." *LONANG Institute*, n.d. Accessed April 7, 2018. https://lonang.com/library/organic/1765-sac/.

"Rutherford's 'Lex, Rex' – Summary." *Reformed Libertarian*, April 12, 2017. Accessed April 4, 2018. http://reformedlibertarian.com/articles/theology/rutherfords-lex-rex-summary/.

"Samuel Rutherford (1600-1661) by Dr. Joel Beeke and Randall J. Pederson." Accessed May 1, 2018. https://www.monergism.com/thethreshold/articles/onsite/meetthepuritans/samuelrutherford.html.

"Selected Political Works of John Milton." Accessed October 20, 2018. http://www.constitution.org/milton/milton.htm.

"Self-Studies." LONANG Institute, n.d. Accessed April 7, 2018. https://lonang.com/commentaries/foundation/framework-of-law/studies/.

"The Act of Union of July 2, 1800." LONANG Institute, n.d. Accessed April 7, 2018. https://lonang.com/library/organic/1800-aou/.

"The Articles of Confederation." Accessed October 20, 2018. http://www.constitution.org/cons/usa-conf.htm.

"The Federalist Papers - Congress.Gov Resources -." Accessed March 19, 2018. https://www.congress.gov/resources/display/content/The+Federalist+Papers.

The Original Constitution, Order and Faith of the New-England Churches: Comprising the Platform of Church Discipline Adopted in 1648. Propositions Respecting Baptism and Consociation of Churches Answered by the Synod of 1662. A Confession of Faith, Adopted by the New-England Churches 1680. Reprinted for A. Lyman, 1808. https://books.google.com/books?id=zCkPAAAAIAAJ.

The Philadelphia Confession of Faith. Sovereign Grace Publishers, 2002. https://books.google.com/books?id=IBzrjAY-UX0C.

The Reformed Presbyterian Magazine. Jan. 1855-July 1858, 1862-76, 1864. https://books.google.com/books?id=qy4EAAAAQAAJ.

"U.S. Articles of Confederation (1781)." LONANG Institute, n.d. Accessed April 7, 2018. https://lonang.com/library/organic/1781-ac/.

"Virginia Declaration of Rights (1776)." LONANG Institute, n.d. Accessed April 7, 2018. https://lonang.com/library/organic/1776-vdr/.

Preface to *Lex, Rex* (1644)

[LAW IS KING, OR THE LAW & THE PRINCE]

THE REVEREND DR. SAMUEL RUTHERFORD

Preface

Who doubts (Christian Reader) but innocency must be under the courtesy and mercy of malice, and that it is a real martyrdom to be brought under the lawless inquisition of the bloody tongue. Christ, the prophets, and apostles of our Lord, went to heaven with the note of traitors, seditious men, and such as turned the world upside down: calumnies of treason to Caesar were an ingredient in Christ's cup, and therefore the author is the more willing to drink of that cup that touched his lip, who is our glorious Forerunner: what, if conscience toward God, and credit with men, cannot both go to heaven with the saints, the author is satisfied with the former companion, and is willing to dismiss the other. Truth to Christ cannot be treason to Caesar, and for his choice he judges truth to have a nearer relation to Christ Jesus than the transcendent and boundless power of a mortal prince.

He considered that popery and defection had made a large step in Britain, and that arbitrary government had over-swelled all bans of law, that it was now at the highest float, and that this sea approaching the farthest border of fancied absoluteness, was at the score of ebbing: and the naked truth is, prelates, a wild and pushing cattle to the lambs and flock of Christ, had made a hideous noise, the wheels of their chariot did run an equal pace with the blood-thirsty mind of the daughter of Babel. Prelacy, the daughter planted in her mother's blood, must verify that word, As is the mother, so is the daughter: why, but do not the prelates now suffer? True, but their sufferings are not of blood, or kindred, to the calamities of these of whom Lactantius says, (1. 5, c. 19) O quam honesta volutate miseri errant. The causes of their suffering are 1st, Hope of gain and glory, steering their helm to a shore they much affect; even to a church of gold, of purple, yet really of clay and earth. 2nd, The lie is more active upon the spirits of men, not because of its own weakness, but because men are more passive in receiving the impressions of error than truth; and opinions lying in the world's fat womb, or of a conquering nature, whatever notions side with the world, to prelates and men of their make are very efficacious.

There is another cause of the sickness of our time, God plagued heresy to beget Atheism and security, as atheism and security had begotten heresy, even as clouds through reciprocation of causes engender rain, rain begat vapors, vapors clouds, and clouds rain, so do sins overspread our sad times in a circular generation.

And now judgment presses the kingdoms, and of all the heaviest judgments the sword, and of swords the civil sword, threatens vastation, yet not, I hope, like the Roman civil sword, of which it was said,

Bella geri placuit nullos habitura triumphos.

I hope this war shall be Christ's triumph, Babylon's ruin.

That which moved the author, was not (as my excommunicate adversary, like a Thraso, says) the escapes of some pens, which necessitated him to write, for many before me has learnedly trodden in this path, but that I might add a new testimony to the times.

I have not time to examine the P. Prelate's preface, only, I give a taste of his gall in this preface, and of a virulent piece, of his agnosco stylum et genium Thrasonis, in which he labors to prove how inconsistent presbyterian government is with monarchy, or any other government.

1. He denies that the crown and scepter is under any co-active power of pope or presbytery, or censurable, or dethroneable; to which we say, presbyteries profess that kings are under the co-active power of Christ's keys of discipline, and that prophets and pastors, as ambassadors of Christ, have the keys of the kingdom of God, to open and let in believing princes, and also to shut them out, if they rebel against Christ; the law of Christ excepts none, (Mat. 16:19; 18:15, 16;

2 Cor. 10:6; Jer. 1:9,) if the king's sins may be remitted in a ministerial way, (as Job 20:23, 24,) as prelates and their priests absolve kings; we think they may be bound by the hand that loosed; presbyteries never dethroned kings, never usurped that power. Your father, P. Prelate, has dethroned many kings; I mean the pope whose power, by your own confession, (c. 5, p. 59,) differs from yours by divine right only in extent.

2. When sacred hierarchy, the order instituted by Christ, is overthrown, what is the condition of sovereignty? — Ans. — Surer than before, when prelates deposed kings. 2. I fear Christ shall never own this order.

3. The miter cannot suffer, and the diadem be secured. — Ans. — Have kings no pillars to their thrones but antiChristian prelates. Prelates have trampled diadem and scepter under their feet, as histories teach us.

4. Do they not (puritans) magisterially determine that kings are not of God's creation by authoritative commission; but only by permission, extorted by importunity, and way given, that they may be a scourge to a sinful people? — Ans. — Any unclean spirit from hell, could not speak a blacker lie; we hold that the king, by office, is the church's nurse father, a sacred ordinance, the deputed power of God; but by the Prelate's way, all inferior judges, and God's deputies on earth, who are also our fathers in the fifth commandment style, are to be obeyed by no divine law; the king, misled by p. prelates, shall forbid to obey them, who is in downright truth, a mortal civil pope, may loose and liberate subjects from the tie of a divine law.

5. His inveighing against ruling elders, and the rooting out of antiChristian prelacy, without any word of Scripture on the contrary, I pass as the extravagancy of a malcontent, because he is deservedly excommunicated for perjury, popery, Socinianism, tyranny over men's conscience, and invading places of civil dignity, and deserting his calling, and the camp of Christ, etc.

6. None were of old anointed but kings, priests, and prophets; who, then, more obliged, to maintain the Lord's anointed, than priests and prophets? The church has never more beauty and plenty under any government than monarchy, which is most countenanced by God, and

magnified by Scripture. — Ans. Pastors are to maintain the rights of people, and a true church, no less than the right of kings; but prelates, the court parasites, and creatures of the king, that are born for the glory of their king, can do no less than profess this in words, yet it is true that Tacitus writes of such, (Hist. 1. 1,) Libentius cum fortuna principis, quam cum principe loquuntur: and it is true, that the church has had plenty under kings, not so much, because they were kings, as because they were godly and zealous: except the P. P. say, that the oppressing kings of Israel and Judah, and the bloody horns that made war with the lamb, are not kings. In the rest of the epistle he extols the Marquis of Ormond with base flattery, from his loyalty to the king, and his more than admirable prudence in the treaty of cessation with the rebels; a woe is due to this false prophet, who calls darkness light, for the former was abominable and perfidious apostasy from the Lord's cause and people of God, whom he once defended, and the cessation was a selling of the blood of many hundred thousand protestants, men, women, and sucking children.

This cursed P. has written of late a treatise against the Presbyterian government of Scotland, in which there is a bundle of lies, hellish calumnies, and gross errors.

1. The first lie is, that we have lay elders, whereas, they are such as rule, but labor not in the word and doctrine (1 Tim. 5:7, p. 3).

2. The second lie, that deacons, who only attend tables, are joint rulers with pastors (p. 3).

3. That we never, or little use the lesser excommunication, that is, debarring from the Lord's Supper (p. 4).

4. That any church judicature in Scotland exacts pecuniary mulcts, and threaten excommunication to the non-payers, and refuses to accept the repentance of any who are not able to pay: the civil magistrate only fines for drunkenness, and adultery, blaspheming of God, which are frequent sins in prelates.

5. A calumny it is to say that ruling elders are of equal authority to preach the word as pastors (p. 7).

6. That laymen are members of presbyteries or general assemblies. Buchanan and Mr. Melvin were doctors of divinity; and could have

taught such an ass as John Maxwell.

7. That expectants are intruders upon the sacred function, because, as sons of the prophets, they exercise their gifts for trial in preaching.

8. That the presbytery of Edinburgh has a superintending power, because they communicate the affairs of the church and write to the churches, what they hear prelates and hell devise against Christ and his church.

9. That the king must submit his scepter to the presbytery; the king's scepter is his royal office, which is not subject to any judicature, no more than any lawful ordinance of Christ; but if the king, as a man, blaspheme God, murder the innocent, advance belly-gods, (such as our prelates, for the most pare, were,) above the Lord's inheritance, the ministers of Christ are to say, "The king troubles Israel, and they have the keys to open and shut heaven to, and upon the king, if he can offend."

10. That king James said, a Scottish presbytery and a monarchy agrees as well as God and the devil, is true, but king James meant of a wicked king; else he spake as a man.

11. That the presbytery, out of pride, refused to answer king James's honorable messengers, is a lie; they could not, in business of high concernment, return a present answer to a prince, seeking still to abolish presbyteries.

12. It's a lie, that all sins, even all civil business, come under the cognizance of the church, for only sins, as publicly scandalous, fall under their power. (Matt. 18:15-17, etc.; 2 Thess. 3:11; 1 Tim. 5:20.) It is a calumny that they search out secret crimes, or that they ever disgraced the innocent, or divided families; where there be flagrant scandals, and pregnant suspicions of scandalous crimes, they search out these, as the incest of Spotswood, P. Prelate of St Andrews, with his own daughter; the adulteries of Whitefore, P. Prelate of Brichen, whose bastard came weeping to the assembly of Glasgow in the arms of the prostitute: these they searched out, but not with the damnable oath, ex officio, that the high commission put upon innocents, to cause them accuse themselves against the law of nature.

13. The presbytery hinder not lawful merchandise; scandalous exhortation, unjust suits of law, they may forbid; and so does the

Scripture, as scandalous to Christians, 2 Cor. 6.

14. They repeal no civil laws; they preach against unjust and grievous laws, as, Isaiah (10:1) does, and censure the violation of God's holy day, which prelates profaned.

15. We know no parochial popes, we turn out no holy ministers, but only dumb dogs, non-residents, scandalous, wretched, and apostate prelates.

16. Our moderator has no dominion, the P. Prelate absolves him, while he says, "All is done in our church by common consent" (p. 7).

17. It is true, we have no popish consecration, such as P. Prelate contends for in the mass, but we have such as Christ and his apostles used, in consecrating the elements.

18. If any sell the patrimony of the church, the presbytery censures him; if any take buds of malt, meal, beef, it is no law with us, no more than the bishop's five hundred marks, or a year's stipend that the entrant gave to the Lord Bishop. for a church. And whoever took buds in these days, (as king James by the earl of Dunbar, did buy episcopacy at a pretended assembly, by foul budding,) they were either men for the episcopal way, or perfidiously against their oath became bishops, all personal faults of this kind imputed to presbyteries, agree to them under the reduplication of episcopal men.

19. The leading men that covered the sins of the dying man, and so lost his soul, were episcopal men; and though some men were presbyterians, the faults of men cannot prejudice the truth of God; but the prelates always cry out against the rigor of presbyteries in censuring scandals; because they themselves do ill, they hate the light; now here the prelate condemns them of remissness in discipline.

20. Satan, a liar from the beginning, says, the presbytery was a seminary and nursery of fiends, contentious, and bloods, because they excommunicated murderers against king James' will; which is all one to say, prophesying is a nurse of bloods, because the prophets cried out against king Ahab, and the murderers of innocent Naboth; the men of God must be either on the one side or the other, or then preach against reciprocation of injuries.

21. It is false that presbyteries usurp both swords; because they

censure sins, which the civil magistrate should censure and punish. Ilias might be said then to mix himself with the civil business of the kingdom, because he prophesied against idolaters' killing of the Lord's prophets; which crime the civil magistrate was to punish. But the truth is, the assembly of Glasgow, 1637, condemned the prelates, because they, being pastors, would be also lords of parliament, of session, of secret council, of exchequer, judges, barons, and in their lawless high commission, would fine, imprison, and use the sword.

22. It is his ignorance that he says, a provincial synod is an associate body chosen out of all judicial presbyteries; for all pastors and doctors, without delegation, by virtue of their place and office, repair to the provincial synods, and without any choice at all, consult and voice there.

23. It is a lie that some leading men rule all here; indeed, episcopal men made factions to rent the synods; and though men abuse their power to factions, this cannot prove that presbyteries are inconsistent with monarchy; for then the Prelate, the monarch of his diocesan rout, should be anti-monarchical in a higher manner, for he rules all at his will.

24. The prime men, as Mr. R. Bruce, the faithful servant of Christ, was honored and attended by all, because of his suffering, zeal, and holiness, his fruitful ministry in gaining many thousand souls to Christ. So, though king James cast him off, and did swear, by God's name, he intended to be king, (the Prelate makes blasphemy a virtue in the king,) yet king James swore he could not find an honest minister in Scotland to be a bishop, and therefore he was necessitated to promote false knaves; but he said sometimes, and wrote it under his hand, that Mr. R. Bruce was worthy of the half of his kingdom: but will this prove presbyteries inconsistent with monarchies? I should rather think that knave bishops, by king James' judgment, were inconsistent with monarchies.

25. His lies of Mr. R. Bruce, excerpted out of the lying manuscripts of apostate Spotswood, in that he would not but preach against the king's recalling from exile some bloody popish lords to undo all, are nothing comparable to the incests, adulteries, blasphemies, perjuries, Sabbath-breaches, drunkenness, profanity, etc., committed by prelates before the sun.

26. Our General Assembly is no other than Christ's court, (Acts 15) made up of pastors, doctors, and brethren, or elders.

27. They ought to have no negative vote to impede the conclusions of Christ in his servants.

28. It is a lie that the king has no power to appoint time and place for the General Assembly; but his power is not privative to destroy the free courts of Christ, but accumulative to aid and assist them.

29. It is a lie that our General Assembly may repeal laws; command and expect performance of the king, or then excommunicate, subject to them, force and compel king, judges, and all, to submit to them. They may not force the conscience of the poorest beggar, nor is any Assembly infallible, nor can it lay bounds upon the souls of judges, which they are to obey with blind obedience their power is ministerial, subordinate to Christ's law; and what civil laws parliaments make against God's word, they may authoritatively declare them to be unlawful, as though the emperor (Acts 15) had commanded fornication and eating of blood. Might not the Assembly forbid these in the synod? I conceive the prelates, if they had power, would repeal the act of parliament made, anno 1641, in Scotland, by his majesty personally present, and the three estates concerning the annulling of these acts of parliament and laws which established bishops in Scotland; therefore bishops set themselves as independent monarchs above kings and laws; and what they damn in presbyteries and assemblies, that they practice themselves.

30. Commissioners from burghs, and two from Edinburgh, because of the largeness of that church, not for cathedral supereminence, sit in assemblies, not as sent from burghs, but as sent and authorized by the church session of the burgh, and so they sit there in a church capacity.

31. Doctors both in academies and in parishes, we desire, and our book of discipline holds forth such.

32. They hold, (I believe with warrant of God's word,) if the king refuse to reform religion, the inferior judges, and assembly of godly pastors, and other church-officers may reform; if the king will not kiss the Son and do his duty in purging the House of the Lord, may not Elijah and the people do their duty, and cast out Baal's priests. Reformation of religion is a personal act that belongs to all, even to any one private

person according to his place.

33. They may swear a covenant without the king, if he refuse; and build the Lord's house (2 Chron. 15:9) themselves; and relieve and defend one another, when they are oppressed. For my acts and duties of defending myself and the oppressed, do not tie my conscience conditionally, so the king consent, but absolutely, as all duties of the law of nature do. (Jer 22:3; Prov. 24:11; Isa. 58:6; 1:17.)

34. The P. Prelate condemns our reformation, because it was done against the will of our popish queen. This shows what estimation he has of popery, and how he abhors protestant religion.

35. They deposed the queen for her tyranny, but crowned her son; all this is vindicated in the following treatise.

36. The killing of the monstrous and prodigious wicked cardinal in the Castle of St Andrews and the violence done to the prelates, who against all law of God and man, obtruded a mass service upon their own private motion, in Edinburgh anno 1637, can conclude nothing against presbyterian government except our doctrine commend these acts as lawful.

37. What was preached by the servant of Christ, whom (p. 46) he calls the Scottish Pope, is printed and the P. Prelate dares not, could not, cite any thing thereof as popish or unsound, he knows that the man whom he so slanders, knocked down the Pope and the prelates.

38. The making away the fat abbacies and bishoprics is a bloody heresy to the earthly-minded Prelate; the Confession of Faith commended by all the protestant churches, as a strong bar against popery, and the book of discipline, in which the servants of God labored twenty years with fasting and praying, and frequent advice and counsel from the whole reformed churches, are to the P. Prelate a negative faith and devout imaginations; it is a lie that episcopacy, by both sides, was ever agreed on by law in Scotland.

39. And it was a heresy that Mr. Melvin taught, that presbyter and bishop are one function in scripture, and that abbots and priors were not in God's books, *dic ubi legis*; and is this a proof of inconsistency of presbyteries with a monarchy?

40. It is a heresy to the P. Prelate that the church appoint a fast,

when king James appointed an unseasonable feast, when God's wrath was upon the land, contrary to God's word (Isa 22:12-14); and what! will this prove presbyteries to be inconsistent with monarchies?

41. This Assembly is to judge what doctrine is treasonable. What then? Surely the secret council and king, in a constitute church, is not synodically to determine what is true or false doctrine, more than the Roman emperor could make the church canon, Acts 15.

42. Mr Gibson, Mr. Black, preached against king James' maintaining the tyranny of bishops, his sympathizing with papists, and other crying sins, and were absolved in a general Assembly; shall this make presbyteries inconsistent with monarchy? Nay, but it proves only that they are inconsistent with the wickedness of some monarchies; and that prelates have been like the four hundred false prophets that flattered king Ahab, and those men that preached against the sins of the king and court, by prelates in both kingdoms, have been imprisoned, banished, their noses ripped, their cheeks burnt, their ears cut.

43. The godly men that kept the Assembly of Aberdeen, anno 1603, did stand for Christ's Prerogative, when king James took away all General Assemblies, as the event proved; and the king may, with as good warrant, inhibit all Assemblies for word and sacrament, as for church discipline.

44. They excommunicate not for light faults and trifles, as the liar says: our discipline says the contrary.

45. This assembly never took on them to choose the king's counselors; but those who were in authority took king James, when he was a child, out of the company of a corrupt and seducing papist, Esme Duke of Lennox, whom the P. Prelate names noble, worthy, of eminent endowments.

46. It is true Glasgow Assembly, 1637, voted down the high commission, because it was not consented unto by the church, and yet was a church judicature, which took upon them to judge of the doctrine of ministers, and deprive them, and did encroach upon the liberties of the established lawful church judicatures.

47. This Assembly might well forbid Mr. John Graham, minister, to make use of an unjust decree, it being scandalous in a minister to

oppress.

48. Though nobles, barons, and burgesses, that profess the truth, be elders, and so members of the general Assembly, this is not to make the church the house, and the commonwealth the hanging; for the constituent members, we are content to be examined by the pattern of synods, Acts 15:22, 23. Is this inconsistent with monarchy?

49. The commissioners of the General Assembly, are, a) A mere occasional judicature. b) Appointed by, and subordinate to the General Assembly. c) They have the same warrant of God's word, that messengers of the synod (Acts. 15:22-27) has.

The historical calumny of the seventeenth day of December, is known to all: a) That the ministers had any purpose to dethrone king James, and that they wrote to John L. Marquis of Hamilton, to be king, because king James had made defection from the true religion: Satan devised, Spotswood and this P. Prelate vented this; I hope the true history of this is known to all. The holiest pastors, and professors in the kingdom, asserted this government, suffered for it, contended with authority only for sin, never for the power and office. These on the contrary side were men of another stamp, who minded earthly things, whose God was the world. b) All the forged inconsistency between presbyteries and monarchies, is an opposition with absolute monarchy and concluded with a like strength against parliaments, and all synods of either side, against the law and gospel preached to which kings and kingdoms are subordinate. Lord establish peace and truth.

Lex, Rex
Questions in the Original

1. Whether Government be warranted by a divine Law?

2. Whether or not Government be warranted by the Law of nature?

3. Whether Royal Power and definite forms of Government be from God?

4. Whether the king be only and immediately from God, and not from the people?

5. Whether or no the P. Prelate proveth that Sovereignty is immediately from God, not from the people?

6. Whether or no the king be so allenarly [solitary, exclusive] from both, in regard of Sovereignty and Designation of his person, as he is no way from the people, but only by mere approbation?

7. Whether the P. Prelate conclude that neither constitution nor designation of Kings is from the people?

8. Whether or no the P. Prelate proveth, by force of reason, that the people cannot be capable of any power of Government?

9. Whether or no Sovereignty is so in and from the people, that they may resume their power in time of extreme necessity?

10. Whether or not Royal birth be equivalent to Divine Unction?

11. Whether or no he be more principally a King who is a King by birth, or he who is a King by the free election of the people?

12. Whether or no a Kingdom may lawfully be purchased by the sole Title of Conquest?

13. Whether or no Royal Dignity have its spring from Nature, and how that is true, "every man is born free," and how servitude is contrary to nature?

14. Whether or no the people make a Person their King conditionally, or absolutely; and whether there be such a thing as a Covenant tying the King no less than his subjects?

15. Whether or no the King be Univocally, or only Analogically, and by proportion, a father?

16. Whether or no a despotical and masterly dominion of men and things agree to the King because he is King?

17. Whether or not the Prince have properly a fiduciary and ministerial power of a Tutor, Husband, Patron, Minister, head, father of a family, not of a lord or dominator?

18. What is the law of the King, and his Power?

19. Whether or no the King be in Dignity and power above the people?

20. Whether or no inferior Judges be univocally and essentially Judges, and the immediate Vicars of God, no less than the King, or if they be only the Deputies and Vicars of the King?

21. What power the People and States of Parliament have over the King, and in the State?

22. Whether the power of the King as King be absolute or dependent and limited by God's first mold and pattern of a King?

23. Whether the King has any Royal prerogative, or a power to dispense with Laws? And some other grounds against absolute Monarchy.

24. What power has the King in relation to the Law and the people, and how a King and a Tyrant differ?

25. What force the supreme Law has over the King, even that Law of the people's safety, called "Salus Populi?"

26. Whether the King be above the Law or no?

27. Whether or no the King be the sole, supreme and final interpreter

of the Law?

28. Whether or no wars raised by the Subjects and Estates, for their own just defense against the King's bloody Emissaries, be lawful?

29. Whether, in the case of Defensive War, the distinction of the person of the King, as a man, who can commit acts of hostile Tyranny against his Subjects, and of the Office and Royal power that he has from God and the People, as a King, can have place?

30. Whether or no Passive Obedience be a mean to which we are subjected in conscience, by virtue of a Divine Commandment; and what a mean Resistance is. That Flying is Resistance?

31. Whether or no self-defense against any unjust violence offered to the life, be warranted by God's Law, and the Law of Nature and Nations?

32. Whether or no the lawfulness of defensive wars has its warrant in God's Word, from the example of David, Elisha, the eighty Priests who resisted Uzziah, etc.?

33. Whether or no the place, Rom. 13:1, prove that in no case it is lawful to resist the King?

34. Whether Royalists by cogent reasons do prove the unlawfulness of defensive wars?

35. Whether or no the sufferings of the Martyrs in the Primitive Church militate against the lawfulness of defensive wars?

36. Whether the power of War be only in the King?

37. Whether or no it is lawful that the Estates of Scotland help their oppressed brethren, the Parliament, and Protestants in England, against Papists and Prelates now in Arms against them, and killing them, and endeavoring the establishment of Popery, though the King of Scotland should inhibit them?

38. Whether Monarchy be the best of governments?

39. Whether or no any Prerogative at all above the law be due to the King, or if jura Majestatis be any such Prerogative Royal?

40. Whether or no the people have any power over the King, either by his oath, covenant, or any other way?

41. Whether does the P. Prelate upon good grounds ascribe to us the doctrine of Jesuits in these Questions of lawful defensive wars?

42. Whether all Christian Kings are dependent from Christ, and may be called his Vicegerents?

43. Whether the King of Scotland be an absolute Prince, having Prerogatives above Parliament and Laws: the Negative is asserted by the Laws of Scotland, the King's Oath of Coronation, the Confession of Faith, Etc.?

44. General results of the former doctrine, in some few Corollaries, or straying Questions, fallen off the roadway, answered briefly.

APPENDIX C

Biography of Samuel Rutherford

Dictionary of National Biography, 1885-1900, Volume 50
by George Washington Sprott

The Scottish minister, George Washington Sprott (6 March 1829 – 27 October, 1909) was a liturgical scholar and pastor. Having taught pastoral theology in Nova Scotia, he returned to Scotland and contributed numerous biographical sketches to the Dictionary of National Biography of 1901. His final work appeared after his passing in the 1912 Supplement. Reverend Sprott is buried at the parish church where he was pastor in North Berwick. —M.A.M.

RUTHERFORD, SAMUEL (1600?–1661), principal of St. Mary's College, St. Andrews, was born about 1600 in the parish of Nisbet, now part of Crailing, Roxburghshire. His secretary says that 'he was a gentleman by extraction,' and he used the arms of the Rutherford family. He had two brothers, one an officer in the Dutch army, the other, schoolmaster of Kirkcudbright. It is believed that he received his early education at Jedburgh. He entered the university of Edinburgh in 1617, graduated in 1621, and in 1623 was appointed regent of humanity, having been recommended by the professors for 'his eminent abilities of mind and virtuous disposition.' The records of the town council of Edinburgh under 3 Feb. 1626 contain the following: 'Forasmuch as it being declared by the principal of the college that Mr. Samuel Rutherford, regent of humanity, has fallen in fornication with Eupham Hamilton, and has committed a great scandal in the college and ... has since demitted his charge therein, therefore elects and nominates ...

commissioners ... with power ... to insist for depriving of the said Mr. Samuel, and being deprived for filling of the said place with a sufficient person.' Rutherford married the said Eupham, and his whole subsequent life was a reparation for the wrong he had done. According to his own statement, he had 'suffered the sun to be high in heaven' before he became seriously religious. After this change he began to study theology under Andrew Ramsay, and in 1627 Gordon of Kenmure chose him for the pastorate of Anwoth in Galloway. He was no doubt ordained by Lamb, bishop of that diocese, who lived chiefly in Edinburgh or Leith, and was very tolerant towards those of his clergy who did not observe the five articles of Perth. Rutherford's secretary says that he entered 'without giving any engagement to the bishop,' which probably means that he took only the oath of obedience to the bishop prescribed by law in 1612, and not the later engagements imposed by the bishops on their own authority.

At Anwoth he rose at 3 A.M., spent the forenoon in devotion and study, and the afternoon in visiting the sick and in catechising his flock. Multitudes flocked to his church, and he became the spiritual director of the principal families in that part of Galloway. In 1630 he was summoned by 'a profligate parishioner' before the high commission at Edinburgh for nonconformity to the Perth articles, but the proceedings were stopped as the primate was unavoidably absent, and one of the judges befriended him. In 1636 he published 'Exercitationes Apologeticæ pro Divina Gratia,' a treatise against Arminianism, which attracted much attention. There is a tradition (which has a certain probability in its favour) that Archbishop Ussher paid him a visit in disguise at Anwoth but was discovered and officiated for him on the following Sunday. Thomas Sydserf [q. v.], appointed bishop of Galloway in 1634, had frequent interviews with Rutherford to induce him to conform, but without effect. Upon the appearance of the 'Exercitationes' Sydserf took proceedings against him, and, after a preliminary trial at Wigton, summoned him before the high commission at Edinburgh in July 1636, when he was forbidden to exercise his ministry, and was ordered to reside at Aberdeen during the king's pleasure. Baillie, in his 'Letters,' gives in detail the causes of his being silenced. Great efforts were made by Argyll and other notables and by his own flock to have the sentence modified, but to no purpose, and in August 1636, 'convoyed' by a number of Anwoth friends, he proceeded to Aberdeen. Rutherford gloried in his trials, but it was a great privation not to be allowed to preach. 'I had but one eye,' he says, 'one joy, one delight, ever to preach Christ.' In exile he carried on his theological studies and engaged in controversy with the Aberdeen doctors. 'Dr. Barron' (professor of divinity), he says, 'often disputed with me, especially about Arminian controversies and for the ceremonies. Three yokings laid him by ... now he hath appointed a dispute before witnesses.' He wrote numerous letters, chiefly to his Galloway friends. After eighteen months of exile he took advantage of the covenanting revolution to return to Anwoth. He was a member of the Glasgow Assembly of 1638, and by the commission of that assembly was appointed professor of divinity at St. Mary's College, St. Andrews. He was reluctant to accept the post, and petitions against his removal were sent in, one from his parishioners, another from Galloway generally. In the end he consented, but on condition that he should be allowed to act as colleague to Robert Blair [q. v.], one of the ministers of the city.

He was a member of the covenanting assemblies in following years, and took an important part in their deliberations, though 'he was never disposed to say much in judicatories.' One of the burning questions at that time was the action of some Scots, with Brownist leanings, who had returned from Ireland and troubled the church by holding private religious meetings and by opposing the reading of prayers, the singing of the Gloria, the use of the Lord's Prayer, and ministers kneeling for private devotion on entering the pulpit. Rutherford befriended them to some extent on account of their zeal. In 1642 he published his 'Plea for Presbytery,' a defence of that system against independency.

In 1643 he was appointed one of the commissioners of the church of Scotland to the Westminster Assembly. He went to London in November of that year and remained there for the next four years. He preached several times before parliament and published his sermons. He also published, in 1644, 'Lex Rex,' a political treatise; in 1644, 'Due Right of Presbyteries;' in 1645, 'Trial and Triumph of Faith;' in 1646, 'Divine Right of Church Government,' and in 1647 'Christ dying and drawing Sinners to Himself.' For his attacks on independency, Milton named him in the sonnet on 'The new Forcers of Conscience under the Long Parliament.' Rutherford took a prominent part in the Westminster Assembly, and was much respected for his talents and learning. In November 1647, before leaving the assembly, he and the other Scots commissioners were thanked for their services.

Rutherford then resumed his duties at St. Andrews and was soon afterwards made principal of St. Mary's. In 1648 he published 'A Survey of the Spiritual Antichrist,' a treatise against sectaries and enthusiasts; 'A Free Disputation against pretended Liberty of Conscience,' which Bishop Heber characterised as 'perhaps the most elaborate defence of persecution which has ever appeared in a protestant country;' and 'The Last and Heavenly Speeches of Lord Kenmure.' In this year Rutherford was offered a divinity professorship at Harderwyck in Holland, in 1649 a similar appointment in Edinburgh, and in 1651 he was twice elected to a theological chair at Utrecht, but all these he declined. In 1651 he was appointed rector of the university of St. Andrews, and in that year he published a treatise in Latin, 'De Divina Providentia.'

On returning from London, Rutherford found his countrymen divided into moderate and rigid covenanters, and he took part with the latter in opposing the 'engagement' and in overturning the government. After the death of Charles I there was a coalition of parties, and Charles II was proclaimed king. On 4 July 1650 Charles visited St. Andrews, and Rutherford made a Latin speech before him 'running much on the duty of kings.' He afterwards joined with the western remonstrants who condemned the treaty with the king as sinful, and opposed the resolution to relax the laws against the engagers so as to enable them to take part in the defence of the country against Cromwell. Rutherford was the only member of the presbytery of St. Andrews who adhered to their protest. When the assembly met at St. Andrews in July 1651, a protestation against its lawfulness was given in by him and twenty-two others, and thus began the schism which mainly brought about the restoration of episcopacy ten years later.

The last decade of Rutherford's life was spent in fighting out this quarrel. A section of the protesters went over to Cromwell and sectarianism, but he testified against those 'who sinfully complied with the usurpers,' against the encroachments of the English on the courts of the church, 'against their usurpation, covenant-breaking, toleration of all religion and corrupt sectarian ways.' On the other hand he was at war with those of his own house; his colleagues in the college were all against him, and one of them, 'weary of his place exceedingly' because of 'his daily contentions' with the principal, removed to another college. He preached and prayed against the resolutioners, and would not take part with Blair in the holy communion, which because of strife was not celebrated at St. Andrews for six years. In 1655 Rutherford published 'The Covenant of Life opened,' and in 1658 'A Survey of the Survey of Church Discipline,' by Mr. Thomas Hooker, New England. In the preface to this work he attacks the resolutioners, and says of his own party 'we go under the name of protesters, troubled on every side, in the streets, pulpits, in divers synods and presbyteries, more than under prelacy.' The last work he gave to the press was a practical treatise free from controversy, 'Influences of the Life of Grace,' 1659.

After the Restoration the committee of estates ordered Rutherford's 'Lex Rex' to be burnt at the crosses of Edinburgh and St. Andrews, deprived him of his offices, and summoned him to appear before parliament on a charge of treason; but he was in his last illness, and unable to obey the citation. In February 1661 he emitted 'a testimony to the covenanting work of reformation,' and in March following he died, in raptures, testifying at intervals in favour of the 'protesters,' but forgiving his enemies. His last words were 'Glory, Glory dwelleth in Emmanuel's land.' He was buried in St. Andrews. In 1842 a fine monument was erected to his memory on a conspicuous site in 'Sweet Anwoth by the Solway.' Rutherford was much annoyed when he heard that collections of his letters were being made, and copies circulated. They were published by Mr. Ward, his secretary, in 1664, were translated into Dutch in 1674, and have since appeared with additions and expurgations in many English editions. His favourite topic in these letters is the union of Christ and his people as illustrated by courtship and marriage, and the language is sometimes coarse and indelicate. He left in manuscript 'Examen Arminianismi,' which was published at Utrecht in 1668, also a catechism printed in Mitchell's 'Collection of Catechisms.' He was best known during life by his books against Arminianism, and his reputation since has rested chiefly on his letters. He was a 'little fair man,' and is said to have been 'naturally of a hot and fiery temper.' He was certainly one of the most perfervid of Scotsmen, but seems to have had little of that humour which was seldom wanting in the grimmest of his contemporaries. 'In the pulpit he had' (says a friend) 'a strange utterance, a kind of skreigh that I never heard the like. Many a time I thought he would have flown out of the pulpit when he came to speak of Jesus Christ.' His abilities were of a high order, but as a church leader by his narrowness he helped to degrade and destroy presbyterianism which he loved so well, and in controversy he was too often bitter and scurrilous (see e.g. his Preface to Lex Rex). With all his faults, his honesty, his steadfast zeal, and his freedom from personal ambition give him some claim to the title that has been given him of the 'saint of the covenant.'

In 1630 his first wife died. In 1640 he married Jean M'Math, who, with a daughter Agnes, survived him. All his children by the first marriage, and six of the second, predeceased him. Agnes married W. Chiesly, W.S., and left issue.

[Lamont's Diary; Baillie's Letters; Blair's Autobiogr. (Wod. Soc.); Crawford's Hist. of Univ. of Edin.; Life by Murray; Records of the Kirk; Bonar's edition of Rutherford's Letters.]

G. W. S.

Rutherford's Last Words (1783 Edition)

Some of The Last Words Of Mr. Rutherfoord; Containing Some Advices And Exhortations To His Friends And Relations, During His Sickness, Before His Death, February The Last, 1661.

He uttered many savoury speeches in the time of his sickness, and often broke out in a sacred kind of rapture, extolling and commending the Lord Jesus, especially when his end drew near; whom he often called his blessed Master, his kingly King. Some days before his death he said, I shall shine, I shall shine, I shall see him as he is, I shall see him reign, and all his fair company with him; and I shall have my large share, my eyes shall see my Redeemer, these very eyes of mine, and no other for me; this may seem a wide word, but its no fancy or delusion; its true, its true, let my Lord's name be exalted, and if he will, let my name be grinded to pieces, that he may be all in all. If he should slay me ten thousand times ten thousand times, I'll trust. He often repeated, Jer. xv, 16. "Thy words were found and I did eat them, and thy word was unto me the joy and rejoicing of my heart." Exhorting one to be diligent in seeking of God, he said, 'Tis no easy thing to be a Christian, but for me, I have gotten the victory, and Christ is holding out both his arms to embrace me. At another time, to some friends about him, he said, At the beginning of my sufferings I had mine own fears like another sinful man lest I should faint, and not be carried creditably through; and I laid this before the Lord: and as sure as he ever spake to me in his word, as his spirit witnessed to my heart, "he had accepted my suffering, he said to me, fear not: the outgate shall be simply matter of praise." I said to the Lord, if he should slay me five thousand times five thousand times, I would trust in him; and I spake it with much trembling, fearing I should not make my putt good. But as really as ever he spoke to me by his Spirit, he witnessed unto my heart, "that his grace should be sufficient." The last Tuesday night, before his death, being much weighted with the state of the public, he had that expression, "Terror hath taken hold on me, because of his dispensations." And after falling upon his own condition, he said, I disclaim all that ever he made me will or do, and look on it as defiled and imperfect, as coming from me; and I take me to Christ for sanctification, as well as justification; and repeating these words, "He is made of God to me, wisdom, righteousness, sanctification and redemption;" he added, I close with it, let him be so, he is my All, in all this. On March the seventeenth, three gentlewomen coming to see him; after exhorting them to read the word, and be frequent in prayer, and much in communion with God, he said, My honourable Master and lovely Lord, my great and royal King, hath not a match in heaven or in earth; I have my own guiltiness like another sinful man, but he hath pardoned, loved, and washed, and given me "Joy unspeakable, and full of glory." I repent not that ever I owned his cause. These whom ye call Protesters, are the witnesses of Jesus Christ; I hope never to depart from that cause, nor side with these that have burnt the causes of God's wrath. They have broken their covenant oftener than once or twice: but I believe, "The Lord will build Zion, and repair the waste places of Jacob." O! to obtain mercy, to wrestle with God for their salvation. As for this Presbytery, it hath stood in opposition to me these years past: I have my record in heaven; I had no particular end in view, but was seeking the honour of God, the thriving of the gospel in this place, and the good of the new college, that society which I have left upon the Lord: what personal wrongs they have done to me, and what grief they have occasioned to me, I heartily forgive them; and desire mercy to wrestle with God, for mercy to them and all their salvation. The same day, Mr. James M'Gill, Mr. John Wardlaw, Mr. William Violant, and Mr. Alexander Wedderburn, (all members of the same presbytery with him) coming to visit him, he made them heartily welcome, and said, My Lord and Master is the chief of ten thousand of thousands, none is comparable to him in heaven or in earth. Dear brethren, do all for him; pray for

Christ, preach for Christ, feed the flock committed to your charge for Christ, do all for Christ; beware of men-pleasing, there is too much of it among us. Dear brethren, you know I have had my own grievances among you of this presbytery. He, before whom I stand, knows it was not my particular, but the interest of Jesus Christ, and the thriving of the gospel, I was seeking. What griefs or wrongs you have done me, I heartily forgive, as I desire to be forgiven of Christ. The new college hath broke my heart, and I can say nothing of it, but I have left it upon the Lord of the house; and it hath been, and still is, my desire, that he may dwell in this society, and that the youths may be fed with sound knowledge. This is a divided visit of the presbytery, and I know so much the less what to say. After this, he said, Dear brethren, it may seem a presumption in me, a particular man, to send a commission to a presbytery; and Mr. M'Gill replying, It was no presumption: he continued, Dear brethren, take a commission from me, a dying man, to them, to appear for God and his cause, and adhere to the doctrine of the covenant, and have a care of the flock committed to their charge. Let them feed the flock out of love, preach for God, visit and catechise for God, and do all for God. Beware of manpleasing: the chief Shepherd will appear shortly; and tell them from me, dear brethren, that all the personal griefs and wrongs they have done to me, I do cordially and freely forgive them: but for the business of the new college, I have left that upon the Lord: let them see to it, my soul desires the Lord to dwell in that society, and that himself may feed the youths. I have been a sinful man, and have had my failings, but my Lord hath pardoned and accepted my labours. I adhere to the cause and covenant, and mind never to depart from that protestation against the controverted assemblies. I am the man I was. I am still for keeping the government of the kirk of Scotland intire, and would not for a thousand worlds, have had the least finger of an hand in burning of the causes of God's wrath. O! For grace to wrestle with God for their salvation, who have done it; and Mr. Violant having prayed, at his desire, as they took their leave, he renewed his charge to them, "to feed the flock out of love." The next morning, as he recovered out of fainting, in which they, who looked on expected his dissolution, he said, I feel, I feel, I believe in joy, and rejoice; I feed on

Manna. The worthy and famous Mr. Robert Blair, whose praise is in the gospel, through all this church, being with him, [I must tell the reader, our author had this man in high esteem, and lived in near friendship and love with him to the day of his death. A reverend minister, lately fallen asleep, that was often with Mr. Rutherfoord told me, he used to call Mr. Blair a worthy man of God] As Mr. Rutherfoord took a little wine in a spoon, to refresh himself, being very weak, Mr. Blair said to him, Ye feed on dainties in heaven, and think nothing of our cordials on earth; he answered, They are all but dung, yet they are Christ's creatures, and out of obedience to command, I take them; adding, my eyes shall see my Redeemer, I know he shall stand the last day upon the earth, and I shall be caught up in the clouds to meet him in the air, and I shall be ever with him, and what would you have more, there is an end; and stretching out his hand over, again reply'd, there is an end. A little after, he said, I have been a wretched sinful man, but I stand at the best pass that ever a man did, Christ is mine, and I am his; and spake much of the white stone, and the new name. Mr. Blair, who loved to hear Christ commended, with all his heart, said to him again, What think ye now of Christ? to which he replied, I shall live and adore him: glory, glory, to my Creator, and to my Redeemer for ever: glory shines in Immanuel's land. In the afternoon of that day, he said, O! that all my brethren, in the public, may know what a Master I have served, and what peace I have this day: 'I shall sleep in Christ, and when I awake, I shall be satisfied with his likeness.' And he said, This night shall close the door, and put my anchor within the vail, and I shall go away in a sleep, by five of the clock in the morning: which exactly fell out according as he had told that night, though he was very weak, he had often his expression, O for arms to embrace him; O for a well tuned harp. And he exhorted Dr. Colvil (a man that complied with Episcopacy afterwards) to adhere to the government of the kirk of Scotland, and to the doctrine of the covenant; and to have a care that youth were fed with sound knowledge; and exprest his desire, that Christ, might dwell in that society, and that vice and profaneness might be borne down: and the doctor being a professor in the new college, he told him, That he heartily forgave him all offence he had done him. He spake likewise to Mr. Honeyman, who came to see him, (the man, who afterward not only submitted to the Episcopal government, but wrote in defence of it, and was made Bishop of Orkney) and desired him to tell the presbytery to appear for God and his cause, and covenant, saying, The case is not desperate, let them be in their duty. And directing his speech to Dr. Colvil, and Mr. Honeyman, he said, Stick to it. Ye may think it an easy thing in me, a dying man, that is now going out of the reach of all that man can do, but he, before whom I stand, knows I dare advise no colleague or brother to do what I would not cordially do myself, upon all hazard: and as for the causes of God's wrath, that men have now condemned; tell Mr. James Wood from me, that I had rather lay my head down on a scaffold, and suffer it to be chopped off many times, were it possible, before I had passed from them. And to Mr. Honeyman he said, Tell Mr. James Wood from me, I heartily forgive him all wrongs he has done me; and desire him from me, to declare himself the man that he is, still for the government of the church of Scotland. And truly Mr. Rutherfoord was not deceived in him, for the learned, pious, and worthy Mr. Wood was true and faithful to the presbyterian government; nothing could bow him to comply, in the least degree, with the abjured prelacy; so far from that, that apostasy and treachery of others, whom he had too much trusted, broke his upright spirit, especially the aggravated defection and perfidy of one whom he termed Judas, Demas, and Gehazi, concentred in one, after he found what part he acted to the church of Scotland, under trust. For this Mr. Wood went to the grave a man of sorrows, and left his testimony behind him, to the work of God in this land, which has been in print a long time ago. I owe this piece of justice to the memory of this great man: and to shew that the only differences betwixt Mr. Rutherfoord and him, were occasioned by Mr. Wood's joining with the promoters of the public resolutions of that time, but Mr. Rutherfoord ever spoke of him with regard, and as a good man whom he loved. After, when some spoke to Mr. Rutherfoord of his former painfulness and faithfulness in the work of God, he said, I disclaim all that, the port I would be at is redemption and forgiveness, through his blood. Thou shalt shew me the path of life, in thy sight is fulness of joy. There is nothing now betwixt me and the resurrection; 'But today thou shalt be with me in paradise:'

Mr. Blair saying, Shall I praise the Lord for all the mercies he has done for you, and is to do? He answered, O for a well-tuned harp. To his child he said, I have again left you upon the Lord; it may be you will tell this to others, That the lines are fallen to me in pleasant places, I have a goodly heritage: I bless the Lord that gave me counsel.

About the Author

The editor and author of this volume, Michael Anthony Milton (PhD, University of Wales; B.A., MidAmerica Nazarene University; M.Div., Knox Theological Seminary; MPA, University of North Carolina at Chapel Hill), is an American Presbyterian minister, educator, and composer. Dr. Milton's education and background come together to support the product you have before you.

In 2018, he retired as a Colonel after thirty-two years of service to the US Armed Forces (Navy and Army). During that time he served as both a top-secret Navy linguist in the Cold War and as an Army Chaplain. Milton studied public administration at the University of North Carolina at Chapel Hill. He completed the PhD at the University of Wales, Lampeter (formerly St. David's College). The author's research was at the intersection of historical theology and pastoral praxis in the public square. Milton's scholarship in public administration, policy, seventeenth-century English civil and ecclesiastical history, ethics, and pastoral theology converge to help recover Rutherford's monumental work for a new generation. Dr. Michael A. Milton is the president of the D. James Kennedy Institute for Reformed Leadership, Faith for Living, Inc., and he was named the James Ragsdale Chair of Missions and Evangelism at Erskine Theological Seminary in 2015. Formerly, Milton was the President and Chancellor of Reformed Theological Seminary after pastoral service that included Senior Minister of the historic First Presbyterian Church of Chattanooga, and founding pastor of three congregations (KS, GA, and NC). In 2018 Michael A. Milton was awarded the *Legion of Merit* by the Army and was honored with the *Order of the Long Leaf Pine*, for public service to North Carolina, conferred by the Governor of North Carolina.

Parents and grandparents, Mike and Mae Milton make their home in North Carolina.

www.ingramcontent.com/pod-product-compliance
Lightning Source LLC
Chambersburg PA
CBHW071130280326
41935CB00010B/1171